The Impact of Christian Mission on the Socio-Cultural Life of the Bhil Tribe in Rajasthan

The Impact of Christian Mission on the Socio-Cultural Life of the Bhil Tribe in Rajasthan

Alexander T. Daniel

South Asia Leadership Training and
Development Centre (SALT DC)

2012

The Impact of Christian Mission on the Socio-Cultural Life of the Bhil Tribe in Rajasthan – Jointly published by the Rev. Dr. Ashish Amos of Indian Society for Promoting Christian Knowledge (ISPCK), Post Box 1585, 1654 Madarsa Road, Kashmere Gate, Delhi-110006 and the South Asia Leadership Training & Development Centre (SALT DC) Jhiriya, Pipariya, Hoshangabad, Madhya Pradesh.

© Author, 2012

> ### *Note for Senate of Serampore College Book*
> "That the book in its original form is the thesis submitted to the Senate of Serampore College, towards the M.Th. degree and is published with written permission. The candidate is responsible for the title, contents and opinions expressed in it.

ISBN: 978-81-8465-226-0

Laser typeset by **ISPCK,** Post Box 1585,
1654 Madarsa Road, Kashmere Gate, Delhi-110006
Tel: 23866322, 23866323
e-mail–ashish@ispck.org.in   •   ella@ispck.org.in
website-www.ispck.org.

Dedication

This book is dedicated to
Dr. P. G. Vargis,
Founder President of
Indian Evangelical Team (IET)
and
South Asia Leadership Training and
Development Center (SALT DC)
in recognition of his immense contribution
towards Christian Ministry.

Contents

Dedication v

Acknowledgements ix

List of Abbreviations xi

Introduction xiii

Chapter 1 Origin and History of the Bhil Tribe 1

Chapter 2 Socio-Cultural Life of the Bhils 23

Chapter 3 An Analysis of Christian Mission
among the Bhil Tribe 51

Chapter 4 Social and Cultural Impact of
Christian Mission on the Bhil Tribe 83

Conclusion 104

Appendix – Maps 1 and 2 107

Bibliography 109

Acknowledgements

I am grateful to the following individuals for providing me with the inspiration to create this book:

Rev. Dr. P. G. Vargis and Indian Evangelical Team for not only sponsoring me and my family for my studies, but also for enabling me to publish my thesis as a book.

Rev. Dr. Aby Vargis for his motivation, guidance and encouragement from the time I met him in 2005.

Rev. K. Sam George, Director, Training Department, IET; Rev. V. D. John, Principal, SALT DC; and all my colleagues at SALT DC for their prayers and moral support.

Dr. Marina Behera has been the ideal thesis supervisor for me. Her sage advice, insightful criticisms and patient encouragement aided my research work in innumerable ways.

Dr. Geoffrey A. Oddie for going through my research work, asking critical questions and bringing many photocopies of rare articles from overseas libraries and Dr. John C. B. Webster and Rev. Dr. George Oommen for their unwavering support and timely advices.

Rev. Dr. P. T. George and Rev. (Dr). Sunny Pappan for their steadfast support and guidance.

All the librarians at United Theological College, Bangalore; Dharmaram Vidya Kshetram, Bangalore; Tribal Research Institute, Udaipur; and Mohan Lal Sukhadia University, Udaipur.

Brotherhood of the Ascended Christ, Delhi, for their support.

Pastor Amos Singh from Udaipur, Pastor Lazrus Patel from Banswara and Pastor Anil T. Baby from Delhi for helping me in different ways during the course of my research.

Mrs. Nola Oddie and Rev. Samadanam for editing and proofreading my research work.

My parents for always trusting me and motivating me to do the impossible.

My brother-in-law Vince K. Zakaria for his encouragement and support.

Finally, my wife Femin for supporting and giving me strength and my children Arpitha and Abishek for being patient during the course of my research.

Above all, God the Almighty for his amazing, abounding grace.

Alexander T. Daniel

List of Abbreviations

CMS   Church Missionary Society
CNI   Church of North India
MBC   Mewar Bhil Corps
SPG   Society for Propagation of the Gospel

Introduction

Historically, the Bhils are the original inhabitants who ruled different territories of Rajasthan.[1] Eventually, the Aryan invasion and later the Rajputs and Marathas subjugated and forced them into the hills of the Aravali ranges. The local princes and landlords made their life miserable through various forms of exploitation like money lending and forced labour. Later, the British officials who controlled the ruling chiefs through their political agents treated Bhils as 'wild tribes' and imposed restrictions on them.

In 1880, when Church Missionary Society (CMS) began its work among the Bhils in Udaipur, Rajasthan, the Bhils were highly oppressed and marginalised people. Exploited by successive immigrants, the Bhils initially did not trust the missionaries. Gradually, the compassion-filled lives of the missionaries and their work motivated them to accept Christianity. The missionaries helped them to improve their social dignity through education and other philanthropic works.

---

[1] The Bhils have a long history going as far back as the 6th century AD. Anthropologists believe that the word "Bhil" is derived from the Dravidian word "bil" or "vil", meaning a bow. According to 1981 Census, Bhil is one of the largest tribe in India numbering around 74,00,459 with 18,40,966 in Rajasthan. They spread over a large territory of Western India and are concentrated in Southern Rajasthan, Western Madhya Pradesh, Gujarat and Northern Maharastra. In Rajasthan, Bhil chiefs ruled territories like Dungariya (Dungarpur), Bansia (Banswara), Deova (Udaipur) and Kotah (Kota). N. N. Vyas, "Bhil," *Encyclopaedic Profile of Indian Tribes*, edited by Sachchidananda and R.R. Prasad, vol.1 (New Delhi: Discovery Publishing House, 1996): 98-101.

However, the integrity and work of the missionaries were always questioned by Hindu rulers and government officials. Often the missionaries in Udaipur were blamed, as in the Niyogi Commission (1954) of Madhya Pradesh,[2] for their cooperation with British administration, meddling in politics, denationalising converts, offering baits for conversion and using medical and educational institutions as means of conversion. The Committee's report states that "...the missionaries have throughout claimed that they (tribals) are not Hindus. A continuous attempt has been made by these (Christian) organizations to foster a sense of separateness amongst the tribes from the rest of the Hindus."[3] The Report further highlights that conversions and the distinction between tribals and Hindus were made by the missionaries with the help of British administration and foreign currency. It also alleges that Christianity has destroyed the socio-cultural heritage of the tribals through conversion.

The purpose of this study is to critically analyse the activities of the CMS mission and the development of Christianity among the Bhils of Udaipur and to investigate the role and impact of Christianity in the socio-religious and cultural life of the Bhils.[4] Considering the report of the Niyogi Committee, the writer attempts to investigate whether the conversion or the expansion of Christianity among the Bhils of Rajasthan was due to force or some financial offers given

---

[2] Niyogi Commission Report's evaluation of Christian missionary activity in Madhya Pradesh is relevant for this study, as similar arguments were made against the missionaries in Udaipur, Rajasthan, too.

[3] *Report of the Christian Missionary Activities Enquiry Committee Madhya Pradesh 1956* vol.1 (Nagpur Government Printing, 1956), 26. This report is commonly known as Niyogi Commission Report.

[4] The Bhils' interaction with different groups, such as Hindus, socio-religious movements and different modern development programmes caused much socio-cultural changes in Bhil society and one of the important agents of socio-cultural change in Bhil society was the Christian missionary activities of Anglican missionaries of Bhil Mission in Udaipur, Rajasthan.

by missionaries or British officials. Tracing the history critically, the writer also intends to find out the contributions made by the missionaries for the transformation, self-identity and self-understanding of the Bhils.

The CMS mission among the Bhils covered the present three states of Rajasthan, Madhya Pradesh and Gujarat. This study is limited to the Christian missionary work done among the Bhils of Udaipur, Rajasthan, by the CMS mission from 1880 to 1954.[5] This study is further limited to the socio-cultural and historical background of the Bhils in Udaipur, Rajasthan, to try to understand how they encountered and responded to Christianity.

A historical analysis of the CMS mission in the light of the socio-cultural life of the Bhils is made through missionary discourses (CMS reports, minutes and proceedings), people's discourses (written documents by Bhil Christians and personal interviews) and other discourses (published works on the Bhil mission).

This study mainly employs missionary discourses. The statistics of Bhil converts is not available, as the Bhil Church of Kherwara maintains no record of their baptisms and marriages of the intended research period.[6] The early Christians do not have much writing about their early history. The writer also used books connected to the socio-cultural life, traditional customs and cultural practices of the Bhils. Apart from these, the writer has also referred to the

---

[5] It was in 1880 that the first CMS missionary Rev. C.S. Thompson came to Kherwara, Udaipur, and in 1954 the Niyogi Report was published.

[6] It has been reported by Daniel Kala Sua and Immanuel Damor that the baptismal and other church records are missing. Interview with Daniel Kala Sua, Layman of CNI, Godi village, Kherwara, 19 April 2009. Interview with Immanuel Damor, Presbyter in Charge of CNI, Udaipur city, 21 April 2009. And moreover the statistics provided by Missionary documents included the record of Kherwara, Lusadiya, and other Bhil stations together.

dissertations of P. C. Jain, S. L. Doshi and A.T. Cherian, who provides a good understanding of the Christian mission in Rajasthan.[7]

---

[7] Prakash Chandra. Jain, "Social Movement among the Bhils of Rajasthan: A Sociological Study." Ph. D. dissertation, Mohan Lal Sukhadia University, April 1988; S. L. Doshi, "The Changing Patterns of Bhil Life in Banswara." Ph. D. dissertation, University of Rajasthan, 1963; Abraham T. Cherian, "Contribution of the Churches and the Mission Agencies to the Bhils of Rajasthan." Ph.D. dissertation, Acts Academy of Higher Education, 2005.

Chapter 1

ORIGIN AND HISTORY OF THE BHIL TRIBE

Rajasthan is situated in the northwestern part of India and is known in history as a land of kings, while its people are known for their ancient and multi-communal society. Under the British rule, Rajasthan continued as an assortment of princely states under the name of Rajputana with its own Rajas and Maharajas. Independent India conflated them to create the state of Rajasthan in which the Mina and the Bhil tribe constitute the majority of the population.[1]

This chapter deals with some major issues and questions; for example, who the tribals in India are? How are they defined? What is the general understanding and situation of tribals in India? Where are the Bhils located among the tribes of Rajasthan?

AN INTRODUCTION TO THE TRIBALS OF INDIA

India has one of the largest concentrations of tribal population.[2] There are 537 different tribal communities spread all over India. According to the 2001 census report, tribals constitute roughly 8 per cent of the nation's total population, i.e., over 84 million people. Historically, different definitions were given to demonstrate the term "tribe" and as time passed by, the concept of tribe or tribals also keep changing.

---

[1] Rajputana, now known as Rajasthan, was divided into 24 princely states, each with its own rulers. C.T. Metelfe, "Geography of Rajasthan or Rajpootana," in *Rajasthan through the Ages*, edited by Suresh K. Sharma and Usha Sharma, vol.1, History & Geography (New Delhi: Deep & Deep Publications, 1999), 1.

[2] In world tribal population, India has the second largest tribal population next only to Africa. P. K. Mohanty, ed., *Encyclopaedia of Scheduled Tribes in India*, vol. 2, North (Delhi: Isha Books, 2006), ix.

Traditionally, the term "tribe" has been designated for those who live away from the mainstream society in remote areas like hills, forests, seacoasts and islands, having minimal or no contacts with other social groups or race. Nirmal Sengupta points out that historically the origin of the term "tribe" is closely connected with the rise of European colonialism and its "evolutionary race theory" of the nineteenth century. Europeans, after colonising most part of Asia, Africa, Australasia and the Americas, used the term 'tribe' to denote those 'backward races' that according to them were 'less civilized.'[3]

According to K. S. Singh, in the later part of the nineteenth century, British administrators, anthropologists and sociologists saw tribals in India as societies that kept themselves away from the mainstream. This attitude led them to study and preserve them as an ethnic community, impose regulations and special agrarian laws that were alien to tribal ethos.[4] This resulted in highlighting the primitive and backward character of the tribes. This concept is very much evident in their definition of the Bhils in India.

British rulers considered the Bhils as a barbarous community and treated them as anti-social elements. James Forbes, the collector of the East India Company, stated that, "the only inhabitants are a set of cruel robbers, called Bheels (Bhils), more barbarous than the beasts among whom they dwell."[5] Doshi and Vyas comment that "the colonial and

---

[3] The evolutionary race theories in Europe were used to justify the supremacy of the white races. Race emerged as a concept and with Dalton in 1872 expressions like wild tribes; pastoral tribes, agricultural tribes or mixed and imperfect tribes were used to introduce to signify the notion of differential evolutionary achievements even among the colonised people. Nirmal Sengupta, "Reappraising Tribal Movements-1: A Myth in the Making," *Economic and Political Weekly* 23/19 (1988): 943-44.

[4] K. Suresh Singh, *Tribal Society in India* (Delhi: Manohar Publications, 1985), 9.

[5] G. W. Blair, *Station and Camp Life in the Bheel Country* (Belfast: Committee of Jungle Tribes Mission, 1906), 26.

official historians have always described them (Bhil) as 'children of the forest' (Hendley 1957); 'plunderers of the night' (Saletore, 1838); and 'nearer to monkey than to men' (reported by Morris Carstairs, 1957)."[6]

Initially, the same notion of "primitiveness" was followed by different mission organisations and missionaries. For example, some missionaries saw "Bhils truly are (as) primitive" and "childlike."[7] Contrary to the prevailing understanding about the Bhils, G. W. Blair, who worked among the Bhils for thirteen years, comments on the Bhils as follows "Yet, even in those lawless days, the Bheel (Bhil) was a person worthy of being trusted at times. His word was good as his bond, and if he promised protection to a traveler, he would sacrifice his life to keep his pledge."[8]

However, as Andre Beteille suggests, the discipline of anthropology is primarily concerned with the study of tribes as primitive people. Conversely, B. K. Roy Burman, a noted Indian anthropologist, strongly writes that, ".... without being necessarily linked up with the concept of 'primitive', it also refers to societies organized primarily on the basis of moral bindings among kins, real or fictitious, having special prerogatives in respect of definite territories or productive forces... ."[9] Thus different scholars highlight different characteristics of tribals like its political entity, cultural content,[10] the kinship relationship and socio-economic criteria

---

[6] S. L. Doshi and Narendra Vyas, *Tribal Rajasthan: Sunshine on the Aravali* (Udaipur: Himanshu Publications, 1992), 43.

[7] David Hardiman, *Missionaries and Their Medicine: A Christian Modernity for Tribal India* (Manchester: Manchester University Press, 2008), 169,235.

[8] Blair, *Station and Camp Life ...*, 27.

[9] B. K. Roy Burman, "Transformation of Tribes and Analogous Social Formations," in *Tribal Transformation in India,* edited by B. Chaudhuri (New Delhi: Inter-India Publications, 1992), 28-29.

[10] Evans-Pritchard emphasises the political aspect of a tribe. P. H. Gulliver, ed., *Tradition and Transition in East Africa: Studies of the Tribal Element in the Modern Era* (Berkeley: University of California Press, 1969), 8-9; Marshall Sahlins says 'Tribes occupy a place in cultural evolution. They took over from simpler hunters; and gave way to the more advanced culture we call civilizations.' Marshall Sahlins, *Tribesmen* (Englewood Cliffs: n.p., 1968), 4.

as the principal factor that binds a tribe together in an egalitarian society with simple tools, low level of production and consumption.[11]

In 1885, during the colonial rule, the North East Frontier Agency (NEFA) and South Western Frontier Agency (SWFA) were made with some special legal and administrative provisions to preserve and protect the tribal system and culture. The main purpose of these agencies was to deal with tribal issues and problems in the tribal land like exploitation by traders and moneylenders.[12] But these agencies also ended up seeing the tribals of India (as elsewhere) through the lens of the dominant *Vedic* (*brahmanic*) perspective and judged them according to the standards of Western science and technological development.

According to Burman, the word "tribal" appears for the first time in the 1871 census of India as an official administrative term, which was later evolved as "primitive tribe" in the 1931 census and "backward tribe" in the Government of India Act, 1935, and eventually found its place in the constitution of Independent India as Scheduled Tribes (ST).[13] Nirmal Sengupta suggests that even in the

---

[11] This concept was largely influenced by L.H. Morgan and Henry S. Maine. They showed that Kinship relation is the most essential element that binds the tribes. P. H. Gulliver, *ibid.*, 9; Max Gluckman uses socio-economic criteria. Max Gluckman, *Politics, Law and Ritual in Tribal Society* (Oxford: Basil Blackwoods, 1965), xi.

[12] Nirmal Minz, "Tribal Issues in India Today," *Religion and Society* 50/3 (September, 2005): 5.

[13] B. K. Roy Burman, "Tribal Population: Interface of Historical Ecology and Political Economy," in *Community and Change in Tribal Society*, edited by Mrinal Miri (Simla: Indian Institute of Advanced Study, 1993), 176-77; Suma Chitinis, "Definition of the Terms Scheduled Castes and Scheduled Tribes: A Crisis of Ambivalence," in *The Politics of Backwardness: Reservation Policy in India*, edited by V. A. Pai Panandiker (New Delhi: Konark Publishers, 1997), 88-107; Jaganath Pathy, "The Idea of Tribe and the Indian Scene," in *Tribal Transformation in India*, edited by Buddhdeb Chaudhuri (New Delhi: Inter-India Publications, 1992), 49.

adoption of this term in India, the superiority of the "Indo-European" race is postulated.[14]

The 1991 census of India records that 67,758,380 of the 838,583,988 people in India are 'ST'.[15] But the constitution is less than precise in its reference. The ambiguous position of the Government of India on what it means by ST is substantiated by the fluctuation of the recorded number of ST. In 1950, there were 212 ST; by 1967, it increased to 314. In 1970, Roy Burman recorded 427 tribes,[16] and in a book published in 1994, K. S. Singh listed 461 ST.[17] Jaganath Pathy says that to justify the enlistment of communities under ST, the Government of India did make several criteria. The list of criteria includes "tribal language, animism, primitivity, hunting and gathering, 'carnivorous in food habits,' 'naked or seminaked', and 'fond of drinking and dance.'[18]

Pathy further argues that over 90 per cent of the enlisted groups do not subscribe to these features but also the criterion conveys the blatant prejudice of the dominant people.[19] Moreover, as K. S. Singh points out, the Constitution of India categorically equates the ST with the Scheduled Castes (SC), which shows that it extends the Hindu socio-religious

---

[14] Sengupta, "Reappraising Tribal…, 944; Stephen Fuchs, *The Aboriginal Tribes of India* (New Delhi: Macmillan India, 1973), 25.

[15] The tribal population has increased to 67.75 million in 1991, from 30 million in 1961. Amar Kumar Singh, "Status of the Tribals in India," *Social Change* 23/2&3 (1993): 9; Census of India 1991, Series 1, Paper No.1 of 1992, vol.1, Final Population Totals (New Delhi: Amulya Ratna Nanda, Registrar General & Census Commissioner, Ministry of Home Affairs, India, 1992), 15.

[16] Pathy, "The Idea of Tribe…, vii.

[17] K.S. Singh, *The Scheduled Tribes*, vol. 3 (Delhi: Oxford University Press, 1994), 1212-1228.

[18] Pathy, "The Idea of Tribe…, 49.

[19] Pathy, "The Idea of Tribe…, 49.

hierarchical system to those who are considered to be outside the system.[20]

Beteille rightly points out that "the problem in India was to identify rather than to define tribes, and scientific and theoretical considerations were never allowed to displace administrative or political ones."[21] Later, in the twentieth century (in 1992), government representatives along with national and international scholars agreed to call the tribals 'Indigenous People' of India. But their recommendation were not accepted by the Government of India as according to them there are 'tribes' and 'tribals' in the country, but not 'indigenous people.'[22] According to Nirmal Minz, the reason

---

[20] SC is the constitutional term for those who were formerly called "untouchables" or "outcastes" in the Hindu society. In the Hindu socio-religious hierarchy, they are below the bottom class but are part of that religion. Singh, *The Scheduled Tribes...*, 7; G. S. Ghurye feels that the term used by the Constitution of India for tribals as Scheduled Tribe (ST) is acceptable because the concept behind indigenous terms like *adivasi* is divisive and undermines the unity of the Indian nation. G. S. Ghurye, *The Scheduled Tribes* (Bombay: Popular Book Depot, 1959), ix; Hardiman argues that most contemporary sociologists and anthropologists follow Ghurye and normally use words like "tribe" and "tribal." David Hardiman, *The Coming of the Devi: Adivasi Assertion in Western India* (Delhi: Oxford University Press, 1987), 13; But there are many like F. G. Bailey, Andre Beteille and K.L. Sharma who argue that ST cannot be equated with SC because more than the similarities, differences are greater between them. Historically, a tribal society has not been static, and yet it has retained its exclusivity from a caste society. K. L. Sharma, *Social Stratification and Mobility* (Delhi: Rawat Publications, 2002), 166; Bailey makes a structural comparison and says that tribe is a society while caste is only a part of the society. He further comments that tribes are segmentary and egalitarian whereas caste is organic and hierarchical. F. G. Bailey, ""Tribe" And "Caste" In India," *Contributions to Indian Sociology*, no. 4 (October 1961): 11-15.

[21] Andre Beteille, "The Concept of Tribe with Special Reference to India," *Journal of European Sociology* 27 (1986): 299.

[22] In 1984 and 1991, the Indian Delegates at the UN Working Group on Indigenous Populations at Geneva stated that there were no tribes in India that could be called indigenous. And that is the reason why while the Government of India is a signatory to the International Labour Organization (ILO) Convention107 of 1957, which uses the term "indigenous and tribal populations', it is not a signatory to the ILO Convention 169 of 1989, which uses the term 'indigenous people'. Alex Ekka, "Indigenous People and Development in India," in *Indigenous People of India Problems and Prospects*, edited by Joseph Marianus Kujur and Sonajharia Minz (New Delhi: Indian Social Institute, 2007), 265,281.

why the Indian government is not designating several of the tribal population as indigenous is only because of the fear that they have to provide several rights to them.[23] Alex Ekka too arguing on the same line says that government fears to give authority of the land into the hands of indigenous people.[24]

Despite its ideological connotations, the term is used differently in every country. But it has always and everywhere carried a negative implication like relative backwardness and supposed 'primitivism' of their social, cultural and economic practices.[25]

While the ambiguity of defining the term tribal or tribe remains in its place, scholars in order to gain an explicit understanding and to study the tribes in India adopt different classifications based on their territory, language and level of integration, etc. Roy Burman classifies them geographically, dividing the tribals of India into four territorial groupings, taking into account their historical, ethnic and socio-cultural relations.[26] Vidhyarti and Rai classify them into four linguistic families: the Austro-Asiatic family, the Tibeto-Chinese family, the Dravidian family and the

---

[23] Nirmal Minz, "Tribals," in *Doing Christian Ethics*, edited by Hunter P. Mabry (Bangalore: BTESSC, 1996), 18.

[24] ILO 169 of 1989, determines the 'right of self-determination' which means the right of secession from the Indian Union. Ekka, "Indigenous People...", 265.

[25] Jaganath Pathy, "What Is Tribe? What Is Indigenous? Turn the Tables towards the Metaphor for Social Justice," *Religion and Society* 38/3&4 (1991): 21-22.

[26] The regions of their concentration have been commonly classified into four or five areas. Dube (1960) and Atal (1965) have suggested a four-fold classification, while Roy Burman (1972) and Vidyarthi (1977) have suggested a five-fold classification on the basis of the regional distribution of the tribal population. But the later writing of Roy Burman also suggests six geographical classifications. Buddhadeb Chaudhuri, *Tribal Transformation in India*, vol. 3 (New Delhi: Inter-India Publications, 1992), viii; Burman, "Tribes in Perspective,"..., 3,5.

Indo-European family.[27] Majumdar classifies them according to the level of integration of tribals with the rest of other people and their culture: 'Real-Primitives'; Primitive tribes, which have adopted Hindu customs, beliefs and practices, but not recognised as forming prominent castes; Primitive tribes, who are Hinduised but maintain social distance from the (so-called) clean castes.[28]

From the above discussion, it can be understood that in defining the term tribe or tribal the socio-cultural lifestyle and racial identity of each tribe should be acknowledged and recognised, as tribal groups differ in social structure, political organisation and religious beliefs. As Sharma comments, the degree of diversity is such that no common feature could be suggested as distinctive to tribal identity in India.[29] But there are some common characteristics unique to all tribes, such as their strong sense of relationship with land, nature worship and their distinctive life. In this study, the Bhil tribe is taken as an indigenous group of people having their own social, cultural and religious structure, based on egalitarian dimension.

THE GENERAL CHARACTERISTICS OF THE BHILS

The term 'Bhil'

The nomenclature and characteristics of the Bhils are very closely related. Their life, occupation, habitat in the forests and other aspects of their life are also related with the origin of their name. The term *Bhilla* seems to occur for the

---

[27] L. P. Vidyarthi & B. K. Rai, *The Tribal Culture of India* (Delhi: Concept Publishing Company, 1977), 68 and 69.

[28] L. P. Vidyarthi & B. K. Rai, *The Tribal...*, 70; Roy Burman says that tribals are of three natures: firstly, they are of secondary phenomenon in nature, i.e., they acquire form and identity from an external source. The other two are primitive and post primitive tribes. Burman, "Tribal Population...", 176.

[29]While some scholars find "tribal cohesion" existing in some central Indian tribes, the same could hardly be identified among many tribes of the North East. Suresh Sharma, *Tribal Identity and the Modern World* (New Delhi: Sage Publishers, 1994), 13-4.

first time around 600 C.E.[30] Most of the anthropologists and sociologists are of the opinion that the name 'Bhil' is derived from their important weapon, 'bow.' Erskine writes that the term 'Bhil' is derived from the root of the Sanskrit verb meaning 'to pierce, shoot or kill in consequence of their proficiency as archers.'[31] Syam Lal says that they lived mostly surrounding the area of Vidhyanchal lakes in present western India and the Dravidians called them 'Villuvar', which was changed to 'Bheel' in the colonial period and later to its present noun form of Bhil.[32]

THE ORIGIN AND DEVELOPMENT OF THE BHIL TRIBE

The Bhils are considered to be one among the many original owners and rulers of the people groups in ancient India. They ruled a large portion of the hill country now included in Rajasthan, Madhya Pradesh, Maharashtra and Gujarat. [33] According to the 2001 census, the Bhils comprise 39 per cent of Rajasthan's tribal population.[34] Mahipal Bhuriya states that "…in the year 57 B.C.E, the Bhils had already attempted to raise themselves from the status of chiefdom to kingship but they were suppressed by the Sakas on the invitation of the Jainas."[35] Their predominance during early times in western India is implied in the fact that the Rajputana, Malwa and Gujarat chiefs mark their bows with the blood of Bhil. It is understood that by doing so they secure a blood covenant

---

[30] Imperial Gazeteer of India, *The Bhil Tribes* (Oxford: Clarendon Press, 1908), 101.

[31] Erskine, *Rajputhana Gazetteers*, vol. 2, A (Ajmer: The Mewar Residency, 1908), 227.

[32] Syam Lal, *Tribals and Christian Missionaries* (Delhi: Manak Publications, 1994), 25.

[33] In Gujarat, the Bhil tribe is majorly located in Broach, Bulsar, Baroda, Sabarkantha, Dangs, Banaskantha and Surat. In Madhya Pradesh, they are mainly found in Jhabua, Dhar, Rathlam and East Nimar.　S. P. Lala, "Impact of Panchayathi Raj on Succession of the Bhils," in *Tribal Ethnography Customary Law and Change*, edited by K. S. Singh (New Delhi: Concept Publishing Company, 1993), 325.

[34] Mohanty, *Encyclopaedia of Scheduled Tribes…*, 217.

[35] Mahipal Bhuriya, "Tribal Religion in India: A Case Study of the Bhils," *Social Compass* 33/ 2-3 (1986): 275-276.

with the early lords of the country and the protection of their priesthood against the local evil spirits.[36] Because of the successive waves of Hindu and Muslim invaders, they were driven to the hilly areas, where they developed their own forms of social organisation and means of living and preserved their characteristics and customs.

Anthropologists and sociologists nurture different views regarding the Bhils. Some argue they are Dravidians, for some they resemble the Aryans and others see them as Hindus. All this ambiguity remains as the Bhils seem to have preserved little tribal tradition and possess no historical tribal literature.

WERE THE BHILS DRAVIDIAN OR ARYAN?

Anthropologists and sociologists like Erskine, S. K. Chaterjee, Y. L. Dshora, Risley and others connect the history of the Bhils either to the Aryans or the Dravidian history of India.[37] On the other hand, C. S. Venkatachar, R. E. Enthoven, James Todd, P. C. Jain and S. L. Doshi see them not only as the original inhabitants of Rajasthan but also as a culturally distinct tribe.[38] James Todd calls them *Venapootras*, (children of the forest) and *Bhumiputra* (sons of the earth).[39] Eriskine,

---

[36] W. Crooke, "Bhils," *Encyclopedia of Religion and Ethics*, edited by James Hastings, vol. 2 (New York: Charles Scribner's Sons, n.d.): 554.

[37] S. K. Chaterjee and Y. L. Dshora see the Bhils as Aryans. H. H. Risley and A. C. Haddon classify the Bhils among the Dravidians. A. C. Haddon, *The Races of Man & Their Distribution* (London: 1924), 107; H.H. Risley, *People of India* (Delhi: Oriental Books reprint cooperation, 1969), 106-116; K. D. Erskine, *Rajputhana Gazetteers…*, 228.

[38] James Todd says regarding the Bhils that "they live where they were born." James Todd, *Travels in West India*, trans., by Gopalnarayan Bhora *Paschimi Bharat ke Yathra* (Hindi) (Jodphur: Rajasthan Prachya Vidhya Pratisthan, 1965), 38-39. The Bhils were given the responsibility of Watchman, as it was the belief that only the most ancient tribe can be the protector of the village. So, it is evident that the Bhils were seen as the ancient and original inhabitants. R. S. Russel & Hira Lal, *The Tribes and Castes of the Central Provinces of India*, vol. 2 (London: Macmillan and Co. Limited, 1916), 281; R.E. Enthoven, *The Tribes and Castes of Bombay*, vol. 1 (Delhi: Cosmo Publications, 1975), 152; C.S. Venkatachar, "An Ethnographic Account of the Bhil of Central India," in *The Bhil Tribe*, edited by J. H. Hutton (Delhi: n.p., 1958), 51.

[39] James Todd, *Annals and Antiquities of Rajasthan*, vol. 2 (New Delhi: M.N. Publishers, 1983), 181.

A. K. Prasad, the Cambridge historians and Syam Lal mentions certain ancient Tamil poets who speak about some jungle tribes in the pre-Dravidian period in the north as *villuvar* (arrow man) and go on to suggest that the reference is to the ancestors of the modern Bhils.[40] P. C. Jain strongly supports the view that there is sufficient historical evidence to suggest that at the time of the advent of the Aryans, the Bhils not only lived, but also ruled in areas of Rajasthan, Madhya Pradesh, Gujarat and Maharashtra.[41]

The historical analysis of sources underlines that the Bhils are one among the earliest people groups of India and that their social and cultural life is deeply rooted in the Indian soil.

ARE THE BHILS HINDU?

For decades it has been argued that the tribals of India are Hindus. Traditions and history have being interpreted to show that they had similarities with those of the Hindus, and therefore had their origins in Hindu religion. [42]

---

[40] E. J. Rapson, ed., *The Cambridge History of India*, vol. 1, Ancient India (Cambridge: Cambridge University Press, 1922), 595; L. P. Mathur, *Resistance Movement of Tribals of India: A Case Study of the Bhils of Rajasthan in the 19th Century* (Udaipur: Himanshu Publication, 1998), 7; A.K. Prasad, *The Bhils of Khandesh* (Delhi: Konak Publishers, 1991), 40. Syam Lal, *Tribals and Christian Missionaries* (Delhi: Manak Publications, 1994), 25.

[41] Except the former Mewar state, the whole of south Rajasthan and parts of northeastern Gujarat and northwestern Madhya Pradesh were ruled by the Bhils. The states of Char and Jhabua in Madhya Pradesh and the present districts of Panchmahals and Dahod of northeastern Gujarat were also the principalities of Bhil rulers. P. C. Jain, *Planned Development among Tribals* (Jaipur: Rawat Publication, 1999), 96-97; S.L. Doshi, "The Changing Patterns of Bhil Life in Banswara," (Ph.D. dissertation, University of Rajasthan, 1963), 18.

[42] The most prevalent traditional narrative regarding the origin of the Bhils is related to a washer man (*dhobi*) who was warned by a fish of a great deluge. He prepared a large box and tried to escape with his sister and a cock. After the deluge, Rama advises them to marry each other and they had seven sons and seven daughters. Rama presented the first born with a horse, but he was incapable of riding on the horse, he left the horse and went into the forest to cut wood. The story concludes by saying that this elder son and his descendants became foresters and the Bhil tribe came into being. Venkatachar, "An Ethnographic Account of the Bhil...," 52; S.T. Das, *Life Style of Indian Tribes: Locational Practice* (New Delhi: Gian Publishing House, 1989), 254-255.

In most of the ancient literature of India, such as the *Mahabharata*, the *Ramayana* and other epic literatures and mythologies, we find the Bhils being portrayed as the ones occupying the lowest stratum.[43] John Malcom cites *Manusmriti*, which says that the Bhils were declared as *Nishada* (outcaste) in the remote past and were expelled into the woods and hills for slaughtering the favourite bull of the God *Mahadev*, which was an atrocious transgression in Hindu society.[44] H. H. Willson infers that in the *Panchatantra* there is a reference to *Phyllis*, which are known as the villages of the Bhil tribe, and in *Jathimala* the Bhils are included in the 'Medh', which is the lowest tribe among all outcaste tribes.[45] Enthoven, while quoting ancient Sanskrit literature of the 11th century, recalls that the Bhils were called by all kinds of derogatory names, such as *Pishacas, Kirath, Pulinda, Chandal* and *Shaber*.[46] Later, when British administrators and western anthropologists started studying the culture and tradition of the people of India, they too depicted the tribals as part

---

[43] In the *Adi-Parva* of the *Mahabharata*, a reference is made of Nishada or Eklavya, a Bhil who surpasses the skill of Arjuna only to be repressed by the command of his guru. Eklavya had acquired great mastery over the bow by practising before a clay image of Dronacharya, the tutor of the Pandavas and who, on the request of Arjuna (one of the five-brothers among Pandavas), unhesitatingly cut off his thumb and presented it to him as *guru-dakshina* (teacher's fee). S. L. Doshi and Narendra Vyas, *Tribal Rajasthan...*, 41. The Ramayana tells of Vail, the Bhil bandit. P. K. Mohanty, *Encyclopaedia of Scheduled Tribes...*, 218.

[44] John Malcolm, *A Memoir of Central India*, vol. 1 (New Delhi: Aryan Books International, 2001), 519.

[45] *Gazetteer of the Bombay Presidency*, vol. 12, Khandesh (Bombay: Government Central Press, 1880), 80.

[46] Around 1st century Gunadhya in Prakreth language wrote a history called as Brathkatha, which was translated by Somadev in 11th century into Sanskrit entitled as *Katha Sarit Sagar*. M. N. Penzer, ed., *The Ocean of Story: Somadeva's Katha Sarit Sagara*, trans., by C. H. Tawney vols. 1-10 (London: C. J. Sawyer, 1924). Speyer says that the original text must be dated between 400 C.E.and 600 C.E.J.S. Speyer, *Studies About the Katha Sarit Sagara* (Amsterdam: Johannes Muller, 1908). Cited by Enthoven, *The Tribes and Castes...*, 152.

of Hinduism. M. K. Gandhi, while speaking of tribals, says that "...in spite of being described as animists these tribes have from times immemorial been absorbed in Hinduism."[47] G. S. Ghurye writes that there is so much similarity between the Hindu religion and the animistic tribal religions that they could not possibly be distinguished from one another and concludes by describing both Animists and Aborigines as backward Hindus.[48] The Niyogi Commission Report also presents a similar view to that of the different superintendents and commissioners of the census department and quotes several sections to prove his theory that Tribals and Hindus are not two distinct entities but one and the same. [49]

Largely, the same idea of assimilation based on the evaluation of Census officials was prevalent in the writings and definitions of tribe in the minds of most of the anthropologists and sociologists in India. When the first census was taken in Rajasthan in 1891, all the Bhils were categorised as tribals under the heading 'religion', but later on in 1901, 1911 and 1921, they were divided into two

---

[47] Gandhiji was speaking in an interview with Dr. Chesterman, the medical secretary of the English Baptist Mission. This article was originally published in *Harijan* on 25-2-1939. M. K. Gandhi, *Christian Missions: Their Place in India* (Ahmedabad: Navajivan Press, 1941), 299.

[48] Although Ghurye accepts the fact that tribals living in the hills and the forests have not been touched by Hinduism but still quoting several census commissioners like J. A. Baines (1891); H. Risley (1901); J. H. Hutton (1931), he says that they are the part of the Hindu society and can be labelled as Backward Hindus. Ghurye, *The Scheduled Tribes...*, 2-8, 7, 19, 20 and 24.

[49] For example, he quotes Mr. Stent, who was Deputy Commissioner of Amravati, who says that when the members of the tribe settled in the Hindu village, they became Hindus and the tribals accepted Hinduism to escape from the taint of barbarism and to raise themselves in the social scale. Mr. Stent, Census Report, Central Provinces and Berar, 1931, Vol. XII, Part I, 329 cited in *Report of the Christian Missionary Activities Enquiry Committee Madhya Pradesh, 1956*, vol. I (Nagpur: Government Printing, Madhya Pradesh, 1956), 29. Stephen Fuchs also says that clans of Bhilala Bhils has adopted Hinduism as a way of upper mobility and are known today among the upper Hindu caste. Stephen Fuchs, "Central Indian Tribes," in *Tribe, Caste and Religion in India*, ed. Romesh Thapar (Delhi: Macmillan India Ltd, 1981), 50.

groups: Hindus and tribals. But from 1901 to 1921, the number of the Bhils in Rajasthan depicted as Hindus went on increasing while the tribals decreased.[50] In the census of 1931, 69.73 per cent of the Bhils were enumerated as Hindus while only 30.12 per cent as tribals.[51] The same procedure was followed in every census and according to the Census of 2001, the tribal population consists of only 12.44 per cent of the total population in the state of Rajasthan. In spite of decaying statistics, the Bhils are still numerous and are to be found in considerable number but scarcely populated areas.

But all this cannot be cited to prove that even though they are seen as an outcaste and lower tribe, they are members of the Hindu religion.[52] Further, it is made clear by Enthoven that the Sanskrit references of the Bhil tribe in the ancient Hindu literature pictures them as a group of people already present in India. [53] Malcom writes that the Bhils are "...a distinct race, insulted in their abodes, and separated by their habits, usages, and forms of worship, from the other tribes of India."[54] In 1874, Dr. T. H. Hendley, who was posted as a doctor for Mewar Bhil Corps (MBC)

---

[50] In 1901, the Bhils numbered 339,786 (about 3.5 of the total population). Hindus as 83% and animists/tribals as 3.75%. "Rajputhana," in *Imperial Gazetteer of India* (Oxford: Clarendon Press, 1908), 115. Mohender S. Bedi argues that half of the Bhils reported themselves as Hindus only because of the work and motivation of the Baghat Movement. Mohendar Singh Bedi, *Drinking Behaviour & Development in Tribal Areas* (Udaipur: Himanshu Publications, 1998), 84.

[51] Ram Ahuja, "Religion of the Bhils-a Sociological Analysis," *Sociological Bulletin* 14/1 (1965): 23.

[52] Morris Carstairs describes the Bhils as "the Anti-thesis of Bhraminical values" because they do everything opposite to what the high caste Hindu does. Morris Carstairs, *The Twice-Born: A Study of a Community of High Caste Hindus* (London: Hogart Press, 1957), 135. Scholastica Kujur, "Are Adivasis Hindus?," *Sevartham* 29 (2004): 107-123; Sudhir Kumar Kujur, "Are Tribals Hindus?," *Sevartham* 29 (2004). 101-106.

[53]Enthoven, *The Tribes and Castes...*, 152; Crooke, "Bhils," in *Encyclopedia...*, 554-556.

[54] Malcolm, *A Memoir...*, 517-18.

conducted a research on the Bhils of Kherwara and with the help of his ethnological experiment proves that the Bhils are very much different from the Hindus.[55]

From the above analysis it can be said that the Bhil tribe neither belongs to the Dravidian, Aryan or Hindu structure nor are they the organic part of the wider society. On the other hand, the Bhil tribe should be portrayed as a distinct entity from the general structure of Indian society. Such a kind of approach has been taken by functionalists and many anthropologists who understand the tribals as a self-sustaining entity and consider tribal society as the whole society.[56]

BHILS OF RAJASTHAN

It is interesting to see the historical developments of the Bhils who once were rulers but were driven out from their own land and called as rebels and uncivilised. The Aryans were the first group who invaded the Indian territory from central Asia and by the period of 2300 B.C.E. they conquered the lands of Punjab, Sind, Baluchistan, Rajasthan and the

---

[55] Hardiman, *Missionaries...*, 26.

[56] Bhuriya argues from recorded literatures that one can reach only to an inconclusive debate regarding their origin in India. The findings of A. C. Haddon (1924), E.W.E. Macfarlane (1941), D.N. Majumdar (1942) and Fuchs (1965) present a confusing picture in resolving the origin of the Bhils through anthropomorphic measurements and seriological studies. Prehistorians and social anthropologists are of the opinion that the Bhils are the autochthons of the Indian sub-continent. Bhuriya, "Tribal Religion..., 275. There are a few other anthropologists like Bose and Ghurye who argue that the tribals are a part of wider Hindu society. N. K. Bose has developed a conceptual frame-work wherein he observes that there is a definite method of tribal absorption in the Hindu society. N. K. Bose, "The Ancient History of Caste," in *The Structure of Hindu Society*, edited by N.K. Bose (Calcutta: Sangam Book); Ghurye, *The Scheduled Tribes...*, 2-8,7,19,20,24. The concept that tribal has their own independent society is taken by Hutton, Risley and O'mmelay J. H. Hutton, *Caste in India* (Bombay: Oxford University Press, 1966); L.S.S. O'mmelay, *India Heritage* (Culcutta: 1910); Risley, *People of India...*, 106.

western part of India.[57] Their life with Rajput rulers was of both cooperation and conflict.[58] Rajput rulers exploited the Bhils for hard and free labour. Guri Shankar Ojha opines that "...the atrocities culminated even to the extent that the Bhils were not only robbed off their land, but were buried alive in the construction of dams and other huge buildings. In the construction of 32 forts of Maharan Kumba (1433-1468 C.E.) and the dam of Gaip Sagar constructed by Maharaval Gopinath, there lay buried the head or the whole body of one or more Bhils."[59] In the Mughal period, despite the injustice and suppression of the Bhils, the latter helped the Rajputs to face the Mughal. In 16th century, when the great Maharana Pratap was running away from the Mughal army, he was given refuge in the forest by the Bhils.[60] Later Rana Pratap paid honour to the Bhils by giving them a status in the state emblem of Mewar in which both Pratap and a Bhil are standing on either side of Eklingji.[61] Besides being partners in the field of battle, the Bhils also had matrimonial and commensal relations with the Rajputs.[62] They, having

---

[57] A. K. Warder, *An Introduction to Indian Historiography* (Bombay: Popular Prakashan, 1972), 3; Stantly Wolpert, *A New History of India* (New York: Oxford University Press, 1977), 24.

[58] Guri Shankar Ojha, *Rajputhana Ka Itihas* (Hindi) [History of Rajputana], vol.3 (Ajmer: Vedic Yantralaya, 1937), 66.

[59] Ojha, *Rajputhana...*, 66. Rao Ranmal of Mandor while acting as the Regent of Maharana Mokal from 420-428 C.E. openly beheaded the Bhil *Gamete* (headman) of Kotda Tehsil of Udaipur District. N. K. Goyal, "Community Development and the Bhil," (Ph.D. dissertation, University of Udaipur, 1970), 26.

[60] James Todd, *Annals and Antiquities of Rajasthan*, vol. 1 (New Delhi: M. N. Publishers, 1983), 264-278. Sharma says that in the medieval period, Bhil warriors like Punja and his followers fought for Maharana Pratap in the Battle of Haldighati (June 1576) against the Mughal Emperor Akbar. Pratap was defeated but the Bhils helped him to run away in the hilly tract of Chawand and Jawar. B.K. Sharma, *Tribal Revolts* (Jaipur: Pointer Publishers, 1996), 19.

[61] G. N. Sharma, *Mewar & Mughal Emperors* (Agra: Sivlal Agarwal & Company, 1962), 88.

[62] The chief of Oguna and Panora named Bhumia Bhil possessed mixed blood from the Solanki Rajput on the stock of pure Oojla Bhils of Mewar. Todd, *Annals and Antiquities of Rajasthan*, 99.

seen the faithfulness of the Bhils, used them as warriors and entrusted to them the task of keeping the roads safe for the wayfarers. Important forts, routes and defense points were put under their charge and many of them were recruited in the states' armies.[63]

During the period between 1748 C.E. and 1888 C.E. the region of Rajasthan was ravaged by the Marathas who ruthlessly carried on their war affairs and their "...march of destruction could always be traced for days afterwards by burning villages and destroying cultivation."[64] Finding their very existence in difficulty, the Bhils desperately put up their feeble resistance to these invaders, which resulted in them being treated "like beasts without pity."[65]

In the early period of the British government, the main problems of the Bhils were agrarian,[66] exploitation from outsiders and the inferior treatment meted out to them by high class Hindus. This always promoted conflict and resentment towards the coming of outsiders like moneylenders, traders and local officials into the restricted areas. So, the British government kept the Bhils under several rules and regulations like restriction of the entry of non-tribals into their lands, etc., which in turn resulted in the alienation of tribal communities from the non-tribal Indian societies.

---

[63] S. L. Doshi and Narendra Vyas, *Tribal Rajasthan...*, 44.

[64] Todd, *Annals and Antiquities of Rajasthan*, 372.

[65] R. S. Hendley, "An Account of Bhils" in *Journal of Asiatic Society* 1875, 369. Grant Duff also reports that if the Marathas found a Bhil in the disturbed part of the country, without any enquiry, he was flogged or hanged. Hundreds of them were thrown from high cliffs. Their women were mutilated or smothered by smoke and their children were smashed to death against stone. Grant Duff *History of the Marathas* vol.1, p.28. Both quotations are cited by Goyal, "Community Development...", 27. Same account is given in T. A. Gurney, "The Bhil Tribes," in *The Church Missionary Intelligencer and Record* (London: Church Missionary House, Aug.1892), 576.

[66] Traditionally, the agrarian hierarchy of Rajasthan is made of different layers. Andre Beteille, *Inequality and Social Change* (Delhi: Oxford University Press, 1972), 22.

Later in Independent India, the SC and ST orders (Amendment) Act 1976, enumerated 12 numerically dominant ST groups in Rajasthan. The Mina is the highest numerically dominant group consisting of 49.47 per cent of the total tribal population. They are followed by the Bhils constituting 44.50 per cent of the total tribal population. The Bhils are largely found living in the districts of Banswara (73.47%), Dungarpur (65.84%), Udaipur (36.79%) and Chittorgarh (20.28%).[67]

CLASSIFICATION OF THE BHILS

The Bhil tribe as a whole cannot be classified as a single tribe because they differ from place to place.[68] From their history, it is evident that the Bhils of Rajasthan went through different stages of civilisation, from rulers of the land to wild hunters of the hills and finally as orderly and hard-working peasants. However, it can also be noticed that the term 'Bhil' is attributed to tribes such as 'Choudhras, Dhankas, Dhodias, Kathodis, Kondas and Warlis,' who do not seem to be truly Bhils[69] and according to Venkatachar, the Bhilalas are also closely related to the Bhils.[70]

---

[67] Mridula Trivedi, *Towards Social Mobility: A Study of the Bhils of South Rajasthan* (Udaipur: Himanshu Publications, 2007), 31.

[68] For example, the social and cultural life of the Bhils of Rajasthan differs from that of the Bhils in Maharashtra. Moreover, it has also been noted that the Bhils of Rajasthan are different in their own districts like in Udaipur and in Banswara. They have differences in their social customs and religious notions. In Maharashtra, the Bhils are divided as Hindu Bhils and Muslim Bhils and they have different social and cultural upbringings. Bageshwar Singh, "The Bhil Are Not a Single Tribal Whole," *Man in India* 61/1 (March, 1981): 91. Irawati Karve too argues that the Bhils are not a single endoga-mous tribe. Irawati Karve, *The Bhils of West Khandesh: A Socio-Economic Survey* (Bombay: Anthropological Society, 1961), 5.

[69] Imperial Gazeteer of India, *The Bhil Tribes* (Oxford: Clarendon Press, 1908), 101.

[70] Bhilalas are the mixed tribe of the Bhils and the Rajputs, which arose through intermarriage of petty Rajput princes with Bhils. *Census of India*, vol. 20 (Central India Agency, 1931), 1, 248.

While describing the Bhils of his time in 1832, John Malcom classified them into three classes—the village Bhil, the cultivating Bhil and the wild or mountain Bhil.[71] Later in 1891, the official Gazetteer of Rajputana bracketed them as Bhils of the plains, Bhils of the hills and forests and Bhils of mixed tribes.[72] Under the ST of Rajasthan, many are from the Bhil groups. They are Bhil Mina, Bhil Mama, Bhil Kataria, Bhil Gametia and Bhil Dungri Garacia.[73] However, the other Bhil groups of the country, according to the ST Ordinance 1950, are Dholi Bhil, Dungri Bhil, Mewasi Bhil, Rawat Bhil, Tavdi Bhil, Bhagalia Bhilala, Pawara and Vasava.[74] Some of the most prevalent clans of the Bhils are Damor, Kharadi, Ninama, Garacia, Kalasna, Katara, Pahgi, Bagora and Charpota. Solanki, Chouhan, Bhati, Rathor and Parmar are Rajput-related Bhils.[75]

Thus, it is difficult to describe and give an exclusive definition of a tribe like the Bhils. In this research, the Bhils are taken as a whole, as there are more similarities than differences among the different clans of the Bhil tribe in Rajasthan.

THE BHILS OF UDAIPUR DISTRICT[76]

Politically, the Government of India has not only declared many taluks of Southern Rajasthan as Bhil Land, but has

---

[71] Malcolm, *A Memoir...*, 520.

[72] Gurney, "The Bhil Tribes..., 577-578.

[73] Bedi, *Drinking Behaviour...*, 429.

[74] K. S. Singh, ed., *People of India* (Mumbai: Anthropological Survey of India, 1998), 70.

[75] P.A. Augustine, *The Bhils of Rajasthan: Burdened by Their Past* (New Delhi: Indian Social Institute, 1986), 19.

[76] The Udaipur District is situated in the south of Rajasthan (also called as Mewar) between the parallels of 23*49' and 25*28' north latitude, and 73*1' and 75*49' east longitude and has an area of 12,691 square miles. Udaipur was established by Maharana Udai Singh in the month of February 1559. Kanhaiya Lal Varma, "Allied Geography of Mewar," in *Rajasthan through the Ages*, edited by Suresh K. Sharma & Usha Sharma (New Delhi: Deep & Deep Publications, 1999), 19.

also reserved seats for ST in the Parliament, Assembly and in Panchyat Samiti.[77] Many districts and taluks were also classified under 'Tribal Sub Plan Area', which promotes development and protection for tribals in Rajasthan.[78]

Kherwara,[79] where the main focus of this research is located (as CMS centre), was not in the British territorial division called the Central Provinces, but in the Mewar state, Rajputana, about 50 miles east of Oodeypur (Udaipur).[80] These states were ruled by native princes, "advised" by English political officers.[81] Erskine comments that before 1850, Kherwara was a settlement of only 50 families.[82]

It is very difficult to give the actual population of the Bhils located in Kherwara, as the Bhils objected to their enumeration when the census operations took place in 1881 and 1891. An effort was made to include them in the census of 1901, which reports them as numbering 2,289.[83] In his

---

[77] Articles 330, 332, and 334 of the constitution provided for the reservation of seats for ST in Lok Sabha and Vidhan Sabha of the various states. According to Article 335, SC and ST shall be taken into consideration in the making of appointments to services and posts in connection with the affairs of the Union of a State. Article 16 (4) provides that effect can be given to the above provisions by reserving posts in favour of the ST. Trivedi, *Towards Social Mobility…*, 40-41. Neeti Mahanti, *Tribal Issues: A Non Conventional Approach* (New Delhi: Inter-India Publications, 1994), 20.

[78] Tribal Sub Plan Area in Rajasthan includes the Bhil territories in which the District of Banswara and Dungarpur, Pratapgarh Taluk in Chittorgarh district, Abu Road Taluk of Sirohi district, Jhadol, Kherwara, Kotra, Sarada, Salumber and Dhariwad Taluks of Udaipur district and 81 villages of Girva are declared as TSP areas. Bedi, *Drinking Behaviour…*, 76.

[79] The name of the place is derived from "Khair," the mimosa tree, and "Wara" a place, i.e., the place of the mimosa or Khair tree. Gurney, "The Bhil Tribes…, 577.

[80] E. A. Gait, *Census of India, 1911*, vol. 1, India/ Part I, Report (Culcutta: Superintendent Government Printing, 1913), 144.

[81] A. Clifford, "Report on the Bhil Mission," in *The Church Missionary Intelligencer and Record* (London: Church Missionary House 1889), 630-632.

[82] K. D. Erskine, *Rajputhana Gazetteers…*, 228.

[83] "Kherwara," in *The Imperial Gazetteer of India* (Oxford: The Clarendon Press, 1908), 275-276.

research on ST, Pooran Mal Yadev reveals that the enumeration of the Bhils in Kherwara has taken place after the great famine of 1899-1900, and it was suggested that the rate of Bhil mortality was as high as 70 per cent. Yadev says that this variation in the Bhil population may be accounted for largely due to the mortality during the Second World War. Actually, there were more Bhils in Kherwara than numbered because, as said above, they were afraid to give details to the census officers and otherwise as mentioned in the topic of 'Are Bhils Hindus?' many of them were classified under the Hindu religion.[84]

A majority of the Bhils of Kherwara in Udaipur District are settled as agriculturists, while those living in the plain have taken menial jobs and are earning their livelihood through daily wages. They still live in scattered areas of their land and follow a unique lifestyle. They build their houses usually with thatch, mud, bamboos, wood and tiles. Usually, the walls of the houses are built by split bamboo, which is plastered with mud or of wood interwoven with leaves and thatch.[85]

SUMMARY

From the above analysis, we see that the Bhils were the original inhabitants of Rajasthan but because of the migration of people groups and societies, they were compelled to adopt the hills and forests as their homes. They have survived a

---

[84] Yadav, while giving the reason, states that the Bhils of Kherwara were afraid of government officials who came to take the census. Many rumours were spread like the government is taking the census so they can select healthy males to send to Kabul for the Arab war. So they never allowed their number to be determined. Pooran Mal Yadav, "Anusuchit Janjatiyon Ke Prati Atyachar: Samajsastriya Adhyayan Banswara Zile Ke Sandarbh Mein" (Hindi) [Atrocities Aganist the Scheduled Tribes: A Sociological Study with Special Reference to Banswara District]" (Ph. D. dissertation, Mohanlal Sukadia University, 2002), 147.

[85] P. C. Jain, *Christianity, Ideology and Social Change among Tribals: A Case Study of Bhils of Rajasthan* (Jaipur: Rawat Publications, 1995), 212.

long history of conflict and cooperation with the ruling rajas and the chiefs of Rajasthan. Often scholars classified them as Dravidians, Aryans or Hindus. But the above analysis makes it clear that historically they cannot be categorised among the above groups. On the other hand, the Bhils are the indigenous and original settlers in the present state of Rajasthan. They do not come under any caste hierarchy but have their own distinct socio-cultural and religious way of living.

Chapter 2

SOCIO-CULTURAL LIFE OF THE BHILS

The tribals in India represent a unique socio-cultural stratum of the country. The social and cultural aspect of a tribe is the essence of human life. To understand a particular tribe, it becomes very important to know their social behavior, which in turn moulds their cultural values.

This chapter deals with the varied social and cultural life of the Bhil tribe in general and Kherwara, Udaipur, in particular, prior to the advent of Christianity. Some of the features of the Bhil tribe remain stationary, while certain elements of it have changed. The primary questions that have been considered are: How do the Bhil govern themselves? Do they have their own religion and customs? What are their customs and practices? Did they have any socio-cultural movements of their own?

TRIBAL ORGANISATION

The Bhils have a unique way of life. It is rooted in the socio-cultural values that they have inherited from their ancestors. They have systems and laws for every aspect of their life. The socio-cultural life of the Bhils is largely based on factors such as territory and kinship.

Bhil Settlement

The Bhils of Rajasthan are settled in two types of villages: An exclusively tribal population and a mixed population of tribes, caste Hindus and other religious groups.[1] The Bhils

---

[1] N.N. Vyas & O.P. Goyal, *Needs, Facilities and People-Socio-Economic Survey of Simalwara Tribal Development Block 2, Dungarpur* (Udaipur: Tribal Research and Training Institute, Rajasthan, 1968), 46.

in Kherwara, Udaipur District, mainly reside in the scattered pattern of housing where all houses are separated from one another.[2] They usually do not mix with others; they live in villages of their own.[3] In Kherwara, however, they live with Bhagat and Christian Bhils as their neighbors. Generally, every Bhil village consists of members of the same clan, but in some big villages, two or more clans may be settled together.

A typical Bhil village is either on a plateau or on a mountain slope. Most of the Bhil settlements of Udaipur are known as *Pal*.[4] The pals are scattered settlements that are essentially a contiguous geographical unit, a hilly region or a valley where the Bhil huts stand on small knolls extending over several miles.[5] According to Doshi, besides its geographical base, a pal definitely denotes a culture and a distinct mode of living.[6] They manage their household with minimal furniture and utensils like one or two bamboo cots, few cooking pots and some earthenware utensils for storage.[7]

---

[2] "Central Provinces and Rajputana," in *Proceedings of the Church Missionary Society for Africa and the East 1884-85* (London: Church Missionary House, 1885), 101.

[3] A. Clifford, "Report on the Bhil Mission," in *The Church Missionary Intelligencer and Record* (London: Church Missionary House, Oct.1889), 631.

[4] A cluster of settlements with total affinity of cultural traits in the forest interior is known as a pal. P.A. Augustine *The Bhils of Rajasthan...*, 19.

[5] Several reasons are given for this scattered settlement of the Bhils in general. Mann says that they have scattered settlements because they always want to keep a watchful eye over their cultivating land and their houses will be built on the spot from where they can easily watch over all their fields and crops. R. S. Mann, "Cultural-Ecological Approach to the Study of the Bhil," in *Nature-Man-Spirit Complex in Tribal India*, edited by R. S. Mann (New Delhi: Concept Publishing Company, 1981), 199. G. W. Blair opines that they live scattered because of the threat of fire, fear of infection in case of plague, cholera and other disease. Blair, *Station and Camp Life ...*, 32.

[6] S. L. Doshi, *Bhils: Between Societal Self-Awareness and Cultural Synthesis* (New Delhi: Sterling Publishers, 1971), 26.

[7] *Battling and Building among the Bhils*, (London: Church Missionary Society, 1914), 12.

Village Organisation

The Bhils have a very systematic administrative system. The authority of their social structure is maintained by the village organisation, which is the most effective unit in regulating their socio-cultural behaviour. This system is led by the headman of the Bhil society. R. S. Mann and Bageshwar Singh state that:

> The political organization of the individual tribe has been assessed in the light of three perspectives; the head and the other leaders of individual importance, the council members who actively participate in the decision-making, and the general body which constitutes the total influence area is subject to the decisions of the councils.[8]

Headman (*Gameti*)

The Headman plays a dominant role in Bhil society. Each village (*pal*) has one *gameti* or chief but if the village is large, then there are two or more village chiefs. His office is hereditary[9] and commonly belongs to the oldest, numerically dominant clan of the Bhils. His primary duty as a leader is to maintain social control and work as an arbitrator in matters of social and economic disputes. As the most respected and honoured personality, all the people of Bhil society seek his advice, help and guidance.

Every Bhil is devoted to their headman, whom they implicitly obey and whose word is regarded as the law. Besides all his traditional duties, he also acts as a representative of the government in the village and speaks on behalf of the villagers to the government on all matters of public concern. The government of Rajasthan had authorised the headmen of some villages to collect land

---

[8] R.S. Mann and Bageshwar Sing, "Tribal Policy in Western India," in *Tribal Development in India: Problems and Prospects*, edited by Buddhadeb Chaudhri (Delhi: Inter-India Publications, 1982), 117,118.

[9] "Some Account of the Bheels," in *The Church Missionary Intelligencer and Record* (London: Church Missionary House, Oct.1882), 591.

revenue and at the village level, the head of the panchayat, the *surpanch*, is also taken as the headman of the village.[10]

Religious Leaders

In a Bhil village, there are some religious leaders who are known as *Bhopa, Rawal* and *Bhagat*.

Bhopa

Bhopa is considered to be a witch doctor of the village. He also administers medicine to the sick. G. W. Blair mentions that it is the duty of the *Bhopa* to find out the cause of epidemics and calamities. [11]

Rawal

Rawal is regarded as the priest of the Bhil village, who performs religious and spiritual rites, festivals, etc. Each village has a *rawal*, whose chief duty is to officiate at the funeral feast (*kaita*).[12] His priesthood has become an integral part of the Bhil society from their interaction with Hindu societies.

Bhagat

Bhagat is the other religious personality enjoying a good status in the Bhil society. He shoulders the responsibility to observe religious rituals for the spiritual development of the people. Besides the headman, the *Bhagat* is also considered

---

[10] R.S. Mann and Bageshwar Sing, "Tribal Policy…, 119. In 1948, Gram Panchayats were formed to establish and develop local self-government in the rural areas of Rajasthan. Though the formation of it has affected the working of the indigenous tribal organization of the Panch in many spheres, the villagers still accept what their headman or the Panch decides for them. Doshi, *Bhils: Between Societal…*, 42.

[11] Blair, *Station and Camp Life …*, 41-42.

[12]John Malcolm, *A Memoir of Central India*, vol. II (New Delhi Aryan Books International, 2001), 179. They offer food to the spirit of the deceased at the feast given by the dead man's relatives 12 days after the death. They live chiefly on alms, and also cultivate land. Blair, *Station and Camp Life …*, 41.

as an authoritative man, and many times, he is also requested to give suggestions and to intervene in matters of conflict.[13]

Village Council

In Bhil villages, the village council is a powerful body having executive powers. The elders of the villages are selected as its members. The chairman of the council is the headman. The council normally meets once in a month. This council makes sure that all is well in the village and resolves disputes and quarrels, etc.[14]

General Body (*Panch*)

The village headman calls the general body meeting. All the villagers except children are the members of this body. Important matters regarding village festivals and other developments are discussed. Y. V. S. Nath opines that the general body reflects the democratic ethos of the Bhil society, where all have voice, but sometimes the headman acts as a dictator.[15]

RELIGION

In 1940, W. Koppers aimed to show that the Bhils were once monotheistic.[16] They knew God by different names, such as *Parmeswar* (Great God), *Nabhavawalo* (Supporter), *Khoro-Dhani* (True Master), *Uparwalo* (One who dwells above), *Bapji* (Father), *Annadatta* (Giver of Food), *Moto Dharmi* (the Great

---

[13] In the village council, a *bhagat* is listened attentively and is also given due respect and good recognition in the society mainly because of his regular devotional life, vegetarian food, clean dress and spiritual teachings. K.L. Bhowmik, *Tribal India: A Profile in Indian Ethnology* (Calcutta: The World Press, 1971), 75; R.S. Mann and Bageshwar Sing, "Tribal Policy...," 122.

[14] Augustine, *The Bhils of Rajasthan...*, 8.

[15] Y.V.S. Nath, *Bhils of Ratanmal: An Analysis of the Social Structure of a Western Indian Community* (Baroda: The Maharaja Sayajirao University of Baroda, 1960), 175.

[16] W. Koppers, "Bhagwan: The Supreme Deity of the Bhils," *Anthropos* 35-36 (1940): 265.

Pious) and *Bhalo Dharmi Rajo* (good and religious King).[17] They believe that the creator and governor of the world is *Bhagavan* (supernatural), who is absolutely transcendental; and his power is manifested both in animate and inanimate things. They glorify *Bhagavan* through sacrifice and worship and believe that *bhopa,* the witch doctor, possesses the power of *Bhagavan.* But later the Hindu religion had a great impact on the Bhils as a result of which they adopted some of their god and goddesses.[18]

In later years, due to the Hindu influence, they started having images of worship but they were kept in open places under the trees so that everyone could worship them unlike the Hindu god or goddess, which is kept in a temple where the low caste are not allowed to even enter the premises of the temple.[19] The Bhils do not keep idols in their homes, except a *paat* (worship items including a coconut, a small piece of cloth and some incense) given by the *Bhopa.* The total concept of the character of their adopted gods or goddesses is different from that of the Hindus. The Bhils worship female deities because they believe that if they do not sacrifice or worship them, they would harm and even kill them. They practically continue to depend more on their traditional nature faith.[20] Jain, after analysing the customs

---

[17] T. B. Naik, *The Bhils: A Study* (Delhi: Bharayita Adimjati Sevak Sangh, 1956), 173.

[18] Bhils have been in contact with the Hindus and as a result, they claim themselves to be the followers of *Mahadeo, Parvati* and *Hanuman.* The Bhils believe and worship many gods and goddesses like *Kali, Kachumba, Indraj, Khodajo, vagajo, Hadarjo, Manatho, Sudhai, Chmohadi* and so on. *Bheru* and *Mata* are also popular deities in the Bhil society. Kesariaji is practically worshiped by all the Bhils of Rajasthan for prosperity and now a temple is made by the influence of Hindu where all are welcomed to worship him at Rikhabdev, 41 miles from Udaipur and Nathji at Nathdwara in Udaipur. Ahuja, "Religion of the Bhils…, 24.

[19] S.R. Sharma, *Process of Social Change among Tribes* (New Delhi: Manak Publications, 2000), 61.

[20] Mann, "Cultural-Ecological Approach…, 122.

and practices of the Bhil worship, concludes that their religious practices "need not be interpreted as acceptance of Hinduism."[21]

Features of Bhil Religion

Nirmal Minz says that most Hindu scholars try to state that the tribal religion in India is not distinctively different from popular Hinduism. He writes "for an outsider their claim seems to be quite correct, but an insider can make out quite clearly that Tribal Religion has distinct characteristics."[22]

Nature Worship

The Bhils are very religious but they have neither a documented nor a structured religion. They do have their own scripture, intricate rituals and a hierarchical priesthood. But usually, due to their proximity to nature, they were generally described as animistic.[23] Land and forest are an integral part of the tribals. They regard trees such as *pepal, banyan, umari, khankhra* and *neem* as the abode of spirits and worship them. They relate their supernatural experience to the material world and thus worship rivers, lakes and water sources in mountains as well. They also believe in the

---

[21] Jain, *Christianity, Ideology…*, 214.

[22] Bishop Nirmal Minz belongs to the Oraons tribal family of Chotanagpur. Nirmal Minz, "The Study of Tribal Religion in India," in *Re-Visioning India's Religious Traditions: Essays in Honour of Eric Lott*, edited by David C. Scott & Israel Selvanayagam (Delhi: ISPCK, 1996), 121.

[23] The term animism was coined by Edward Burnett Taylor in Primitive Culture (1871) from the Latin word *anima* meaning breath or soul. Animism is regarded as probably one of humanity's oldest beliefs that the soul or spirit existed in every object, even if it was inanimate. Lishi Tado, "Donyi-Poloism and Its Impact on the Life of the People of Arunachal Pradesh" (B.D. thesis, United Theological College, 2008), 69. Erskine writes that in, "the last census [1901] 97.25% of the tribe were recognized as animists." Erskine, *Rajputhana Gazetteers…*, 235. F.G. Bailey after reviewing the anthropological literature of India, says "The Tribals are said to be a people 'geographically isolated' who live in the hills in a state of economic backwardness with a distinct language of their own and profess a religion which is animism." Bailey, ""Tribe" and "Caste" in India"…, 7.

existence of spirits and consider the whole neighbourhood whether village or forest as full of spirits.

Nirmal Minz observes that for all the tribals in India, land and forest are not only God's given gift to them but are also their life.[24] The roots, fruits, flowers, leaves, trunks and barks of trees are life-sustaining resources for the tribals. So Cutting off wood from live trees is considered a sin, because they believe that the presence of God inhabits trees, water, stone and so on. Also, for a Bhil, community is of great importance and they believe that nature is not the possession of an individual, but of the community. Therefore their religion is more community-oriented; for example, the whole *phala* (hamlet) rather than individuals offer the first fruits of grains, such as corn, in the *devara* (village temple), and for the common good of all the members of the *pala*, sacrifice a goat or buffalo for the arrival of rain.[25]

Spirits and Witchcraft

The Bhils are generally recognised as obsessed with spirits.[26] Knowledge of the human anatomy and physical functioning of the human body are practically unknown to them. In such a situation, psychosomatic diseases and unknown factors causing illness are attributed to the work of evil spirits (*bhut*) and to witchcraft (*dakan*). The evil spirits who are commonly known as *bhuts* are believed to be residing in haunted places, such as gorges, riversides, hollow trees and water ponds.[27]

---

[24] Nirmal Minz, "Cultural Identity of Tribals in India," *Social Action* 43/1 (January-March, 1993): 34.

[25] D. R. Ahuja, *Folklore of Rajasthan* (New Delhi: Nation Book Trust, 1950), 26.

[26] N.N. Vyas, R.S. Mann and N.D. Choudhary, eds. *Rajasthan Bhils* (Udaipur: Tribal Research Institute, 1968), 16.

[27] D.N. Majumdar, *Races and Culture of India* (Bombay: Asia Publishing House, 1961), 423.

They consider witchcraft to be a powerful method of harming an individual. Any of the offences perpetrated by witches against the village community or individuals are taken seriously and punishable even to the extent of expulsion from the village or chopping off their nose, besides a sound flogging.[28] Witch-swinging was also much prevalent among the Bhils, but by 1861, the authorities of Mewar Bhil Corps were able to restrict it completely.[29]

Ancestor Worship

Ancestor worship[30] has become customary among the Bhils. They believe that their ancestors (*Khatris*) are benevolent spirits, so they worship them.[31] Ancestors are believed to have the power and capacity to protect them from evil spirits and to decide their destiny. So Bhils are always cautious about performing rites and observe all ceremonies without fail because they also believe that failure to do so can bring calamity or disaster to the families.[32]

From the above discussion on the religion of the Bhils, it can be argued that their social organisation, magic-religious systems and adherence to traditional values point to the fact

---

[28] Bhuriya, "Tribal Religion…, 281.

[29]The Village Gametis offered MBC officials their promise engraved on a stone, which was fixed on the right hand side of the main entrance of the temple of Rikhabdeo. Mathur, *Resistance Movement…*, 89. But C.S. Thompson in 1883 records that he has witnessed a witch-swinging which has taken place in Udaipur. C.S. Thompson, "The Bhil Mission," in *The Church Missionary Intelligencer and Record* (London: Church Missionary House, July, 1883), 416.

[30] In almost all the tribal culture, ancestral worship is a common feature, as they recognise that human power has limitations but through worshipping their ancestors, they acquire more power over their unnatural circumstances. L.P. Vidyarthi & B.K. Rai, *The Tribal Culture of India…*, 245.

[31] The Bhils commonly believe that if they do not worship their ancestors, the soul of their ancestors will become a malevolent spirit. Mathur, *Resistance Movement…*, 15.

[32] "Central Provinces and Rajputana," in *Proceedings of the Church Missionary Society for Africa and the East 1901-1902* (London: Church Missionary House, 1902), 228.

that the Bhils in the past had their own religious system. These ancient traditional elements are still visible among the Bhils of Udaipur, Rajasthan.

Festivals

Bhagoria and *Gauri* are important festivals for the Bhils. Both these festivals are celebrated by uniting different villages, so it becomes a time of courtships and matrimonial alliances as well.[33] Doshi observes that *Gauri* binds the participating villages in a network of kinship and economic relations.[34] In addition to these, they have adopted many Hindu festivals, such as the spring equinox (*Holi*), the autumn equinox (*dasahra*) and the festival of light (*deepawali*) on the full-moon in October and November.[35] They later adopted many other festivals like *Akhathreej* and *Shivaratri*, which are celebrated with great enthusiasm.

But the Bhils celebrate them very distinctively and the total concept of celebrating them varies greatly from the Hindu ways of celebration. Hermanns argues that the coincidence, by which the date of *Phalgun* falls on *Holi* and the *Sohrai* festival on *Deepawali*, does not imply that the tribals have become Hindus and observe Hindu festivals. Like most people, the tribals follow the seasons and their festivals are regulated by the phase of the moon, by New and Full Moon.[36]

Moreover, the Bhils have their own interpretation and background for each festival. For a Bhil, festivals are mostly connected with the ancestor-cult. Mann says that "the Bhils depend on their deities and venerate them through the

---

[33] Robert Deliege, *The Bhils of Western India: Some Empirical and Theoretical Issues in Anthropology in India* (New Delhi: National Publishing House, 1985), 122.

[34] J.K. Doshi, *Social Structure and Cultural Change in a Bhil Village* (Delhi: New Heights, 1969), 145-150.

[35] Bhowmik, *Tribal India…*, 75; *The Church among the Bhils*, (Lucknow: The National Christian Council and the Bhil Work Council, 1953), 11.

[36] M. Hermanns, *Hinduism and Tribal Culture* (Bombay: K.L. Fernandes, 1957), 33.

observance of festivals."[37] For example, *Deepawali* for them is not a festival of light but a time to remember their ancestors. *Holi* is celebrated for almost a month; Hindu *Navaratri* is Bhils *Norate*.[38] For a Bhil, the time of festival is of celebration, joy and fun rather than ritual, so they enjoy it by dancing and singing and consuming a large quantity of alcohol.

Customs and Practices

The Bhils of Rajasthan is an important indigenous community having their own customs and practices like marriages, divorce, funeral ceremony, tattooing, etc. But it can be argued that in the tribal culture, customs and laws keep on changing mainly due to their interaction with non-tribal neighbourhood, and so nothing is stationary. The Bhils also underwent many cultural syntheses. Consequently, many variations to suit the local circumstances took place but the most important point to be noted is that the underlying ideas and principles are the same throughout the Bhil region and that they are known and observed by every tribal.

Marriage

Among the Bhils, marriage[39] with the members of the same clan is not permissible. According to their system, as Mann

---

[37] R.S. Mann, "Structure and Role Dynamics among the Bhils of Rajasthan: A Case of Bhagats," in *Tribal Movements in India*, edited by K.S. Singh (New Delhi: Manohar Publications, 1982), 313. The ancestors' spirits are believed to visit the families of the clan on certain occasions like festivals and marriage ceremonies. L.P. Vidyarthi & B.K. Rai, The Tribal Culture of India..., 247. The Bhils have two types of ancestral worship; they are known as *Purvaj rammana* and *Lapsi*. *Purvaj rammana* is conducted during the *Navartri* (a Hindu festival adopted by the Bhils) festival season to prevent their ancestors from becoming a spirit." *Lapsi* is observed by the Bhils once in a year. Mathur, *Resistance Movement...*, 15.

[38] "Central Provinces and Rajputana Mission," in *Proceedings of the Church Missionary Society 1904-1905* (London: Church Missionary House, 1905), 225.

[39] Among the Bhils, five types of marriage is prevalent: Arranged; Capture; Elopement; *Jhagda* (among the married couple, if either one is not satisfied, they can choose to run away with whomsoever they like);and *Natra* (form of a marriage by a widow or a woman who has left her husband or has been abandoned by him). Roop Singh, "Marriage and Law among the Bhils of Rajasthan" *Eastern Anthropologist* 40/2 (April-June1987): 88-92.

says, "…the couple has to fend for themselves. This leads to the pattern of nuclear families so predominantly found among the Bhils… Only the younger son inherits the parental house and continues to stay with parents."[40]

According to the Bhil custom, the Bhils normally resort to marriage by procurement, which is commonly known as *dapa*. The bridegroom has to pay a bride-price to the bride's father. In ancient times, a person who has more than one wife has a good status in the Bhil society.[41] So polygamy was much prevalent among the Bhils of southern Rajasthan as it accumulated additional income to the family through their labour.[42]

Divorce

In the Bhil society, divorce is a very rare phenomenon. Mathur asserts that the, "grounds for divorce for a man are sterility, ill temper or adultery of his wife; while for a woman the grounds are lunacy, drunkenness, extravagancy and extramarital relations of the husband."[43] Widows enjoy the freedom of remarriage, which is called *Natra*. Generally, they are married to the younger brother of the deceased husband.[44]

Status of Women

M. S. Mishkaben narrates that in the early nineteenth century, Bhil women were exploited and were sexually abused by intruders and landlords.[45] But women in tribal societies

---

[40] Mann, "Cultural-Ecological Approach…, 119-120.

[41] Mathur, *Resistance Movement…*, 12.

[42] Though the Bhils are generally known as polygamists, only the rich practice it as they are required to pay the bride-price. A popular folk song shows that there was a Bhil named Nanji who had twelve wives but he found out that their demands were undesirable. The folk song very well conveys that it is easy to practice polygamy but very difficult to maintain an additional wife. Trivedi, *Towards Social Mobility…*, 56.

[43] Mathur, *Resistance Movement…*, 12.

[44] Mathur, *Resistance Movement…*, 12.

[45] Marija Sres Mishkaben, *To Survive and to Prevail: Stories of the Tribal Women of Sabarkantha* (New Delhi: Indian Social Institute, 1996), 12.

occupy an important place in their homes. According to G. M. Carstairs, although the position of Bhil women in the family and in the community at large is marked by several social disabilities, they have better status than the women of the orthodox Hindu families.[46] They enjoy greater freedom of self-expression in comparison to caste Hindus. In a Bhil family, usually a woman obeys the orders of her husband but she has the right to object to any decision of her husband and can even bring her grievances before the *Panch* (village council). All major decisions in the family are taken with the consent of the wife. Both can agree or disagree and express their free will when confronted with decision-making problems.[47]

A Bhil woman in her own home is not a liability but an asset, as she is considered equally responsible for efficient household and farm work. She enjoys full freedom of movement. She goes for marketing, settles deal with the trader and her free mobility does not create any suspicion of illicit relations on her part as a wife. As a mother, a woman has a greater role to play in the Bhil society. She rears and disciplines her children and is highly respected by them. All family rites from birth to death are observed by her.[48]

Tattooing

Bhil tribes in general are very fond of tattoos.[49] They have both physical and spiritual reasons for adopting this custom.

---

[46] G.M. Carstairs, "The Bhils of Kotra Bhomat," *Eastern Anthropologist* 4/ 3&4 (1954): 175.

[47] N.N. Vyas, "Women in Tribal Society," in *Rajasthan Bhils*, edited by N.N. Vyas, K.S. Mann and N.D. Choudhary (Udaipur: Manikyalal Verma Tribal Research and Training Institute, 1978), 55.

[48] Though a woman exercises all the privileges in her social life, she is treated as a marketable commodity. She is bought in marriage by payment of bride-price (*dapa*). Goyal,"Community Development…, 66.

[49] The Bhils mark their body with an emblem consisting of an object, such as an animal or plant, which serves as the symbol of a family or a clan. J.V. Ferreira, *Totemism in India* (Bombay: Oxford University Press, 1964), 24.

Bhils see it as an ornament to their body, as their God also had tattoos on the shoulders and arms. They also use it as a sacred rite by which the body is sanctified. Bhil legend says that only those who have tattoos during their lifespan will be allowed to enter heaven. Later, tattooing was widespread as it was regarded as a remedy for certain pains in the body.[50]

Food and Drink

They like maize the most. It is also the principal cereal of the diet of the Bhils.[51] The Bhils consider that whatever is bestowed on them by nature should be consumed. Among the Bhils of south Rajasthan, the use of liquor is customary. As part of their custom, they consume a large quantity of alcohol on all occasions of life, such as birth of a child, naming ceremony, betrothal, marriage, settlement of disputes, death and festivals. Tracing the habitual nature of drinking among the Bhils, M. S. Bedi observes that *Mahuva* (*Bassia latifolia*) flowers are used to distil liquor, as it is freely available in the pastureland and adjoining forests. They manufacture it with the acceptance of family and the close relatives.[52] Women and children too join in drinking. Jain comments that "the Bhils considered liquor as a food of supernatural, i.e., *Bhagavan*, which possessed an element of divine power."[53] So, it is also offered to the family deity and ancestors on different occasions of the year.

FOLK CULTURE

Bhils' folk culture is a cluster of folklore, folkdance, folk music and art and craft of the people. They have a rich

---

[50] Manohar Lal, "A Survey of the Evangelistic Ministry among the Bhil Tribe in Banswara District of Rajasthan" (B.D. thesis, Union Biblical Seminary, 1985), 6.

[51] They also have dal, wheat, pulse, pea, gram, rice and so on. Jain, *Christianity, Ideology...*, 85.

[52] Bedi, *Drinking Behaviour...*, 26.

[53] Jain, *Christianity, Ideology...*, 89.

literature filled with folklore and beautiful folk songs. Their social life, religious beliefs, economic life, agriculture, cattle, poultry, thoughts and aspirations are manifested in folk literature.

Folklore

Folklore[54] is the unwritten lore or tale of a particular culture that is established through their interaction with nature and human beings. Mathur underscores the fact that "the folklore of the Bhils is full of descriptions of demons and fairies. The fairies are believed to induce persons by their beauty, wealth and all sorts of worldly luxuries."[55] There are also stories of heroes and heroic deeds that contain good morals and are used for disciplining and educating children. These stories are very helpful in educating illiterate people to become active, truthful and responsible.

Folk Music and Dance

Of all the communal activities of the tribals, singing and dancing play the most attractive and important role.[56] Folk music and dances are the cultural expression of the Bhil society. They believe that their sacred dances were taught

---

[54] Vidyarthi and Rai comment that folklore is the mirror and unwritten record of tribal culture, B.K. Rai, *The Tribal Culture of India...*, 247. Durga Bhagvat, who gives more importance to folklore and tale, says it performs the important function of shedding light on some of the vital culture traits of the people like their psychology, their attitude towards the gods and fellow beings, their religious practices and philosophy of life. Bhagvat, Durga. "Folk tales of Central India." *Asian Folklore Studies* 31, no. 2 (1972): 1-89. *ATLA Religion Database with ATLA Serials*, EBSCO*host* (13 Nov 2009): 2.

[55] Mathur, *Resistance Movement...*, 16.

[56]Through the words and actions of a Bhil, not only their recreative utility is most apparent but one can easily find its social and religious significance moored deeply in the local and tribal tradition. If a man or a woman breaks any moral rule of the tribe, the person is debarred from taking any part in the communal dancing, just as he or she is not allowed to take food with the rest. Bhagvat, Durga. "Dances and charms of the tribes of central India." *Asian Folklore Studies* 31/1 (1972): 41-70. *ATLA Religion Database with ATLA Serials*, EBSCO*host* (13 Nov 2009): 41.

by their gods and thus they are of sacred origin. So no rite or ritual is complete without dancing. Songs are used to appease their deities. For example, they sing to get a remedy for a sickness like chicken pox. Clan members sing during the night, while the head of the family takes the child on his lap and sings:

> Kalka mata come from Pawagarh! Please, come and play in our courtyards. The goddess from Pawan has come; And stands at our door…Mata, my children are sick. Please come and play with them in the courtyard. When they are well again, I shall have them married happily, If you are jealous and unjust, We shall blame you, O Mata. Your reputation will suffer….[57]

The Bhils have different kinds of songs and dances for different occasions, such as songs of recreation, dance-songs, songs connected with rites, songs of marriage, songs of birth, songs of death, songs of hero-worship, etc.[58]

Art and Craft

The art and craft of the Bhils are related to their region and culture. In their house, they carve the models of their deity on their doors. They make some kinds of art on the muddy floor of their house. They make baskets, pots, garments and carpets.[59] The arts and crafts of the Bhils are also associated with their beliefs and mystical ideas. They carve the figures of men carrying swords, bow and arrow and riding on horseback. They believe that these carvings help them to control evil spirits.[60]

---

[57] Mahipal Bhuriya, *Folksongs of the Bhils* (Indore: Mahipal Publications, 1979), 121.

[58] Bhagvat, Durga. "The folk songs of central India." *Asian Folklore Studies* 35/2 (1976): 43-80. *ATLA Religion Database with ATLASerials*, EBSCO*host* (13Nov 2009): 44.

[59] "Rajputhana," in *Imperial Gazetteer of India…*, 131.

[60] Mathur, *Resistance Movement…*, 15.

THE BHILS' WORLDVIEW

Culture of any race or tribe consists of two levels: The surface-behavior level and the deep-worldview level. The surface-behavior level is subjected to change due to social and cultural interaction, but the worldview lies deep in the heart of all human beings in the form of a certain structure of basic assumptions, values and allegiances in terms of which people interpret and behave.[61]

The Bhils never travel alone outside their own *pal* and surroundings. They always had the view that whatever is given through nature has to be consumed so they also started perceiving intoxicating drinks as God. As the Bhils considered other professions, except farming, as inferior, they did not attain upward mobility in the area of education. They considered life as temporal, so they never kept anything for tomorrow. 'Eat, drink and be merry' is their philosophy of life. They also have the belief that god can be pleased by poverty, so they tend to live as it pleases her (*Khejadi mata*).[62] It was commonly believed that misfortune, illness and sometimes death were caused by the actions of malevolent spirits, an evil eye or the spells of witches.[63]

ECONOMY

Economy is an important constituent of community life. It plays a deciding role in the formation of the cultural and social structure of society. The first and foremost characteristic of tribal economy is the close relationship

---

[61] Charles H. Kraft, *Anthropology for Christian Witness* (Maryknoll, New York: Orbis Books, 2001), 11.

[62] Abraham T. Cherian, "Contribution of the Churches and the Mission Agencies to the Bhils of Rajasthan" (Ph. D. dissertation, Acts Academy of Higher Education, 2005), 27.

[63] David Hardiman, "Assertion, Conversion, and Indian Nationalism: Govind's Movement Amongst the Bhils," in *Religious Conversion in India: Modes, Motivations, and Meanings,* edited by Rowena Robinson & Sathianathan Clarke (New Delhi: Oxford University Press, 2003), 264.

between the tribal economic life and the natural environment or habitat, which, in general, is the forest. Trivedi argues that the Bhil economic condition was affected very much by two basic elements. Firstly, they were isolated from mainline civilisations; and secondly, they were exploited by caste Hindus.[64] During the British period, the rulers made some changes in land administration, but did not bring any improvement to the lot of the Bhils.[65] Their economy remained at the subsistence level and they subsidised it by collecting wood and other forest products. In independent India too, the constitutional status ascribed to the Bhils along with all the ST in terms of safety and security was based on isolation, which resulted in their poverty, backwardness and illiteracy. Exploitation has remained the main problem of the people.

S. L. Doshi points out that the economic structure of the Bhil tribe falls under different economic stages, from food gathering to industrial labour.[66] In economic development,

---

[64] Trivedi, *Towards Social Mobility...*, 36.

[65] Lower caste members such as Patels, Dangis and Bhois were allotted new and fertile patches of land but the Bhils had to confine themselves to the *Pals* (villages) where they cultivated on the terraces carved by accumulation of alluvial behind *Kaccha* (temperory) dams in the wells of seasonal streams known as *Daras* (streams). Goyal, "Community Development...", 28.

[66] Doshi, *Bhils: Between Societal...*, 54. Vidyarthi and Rai divide the economic development of Indian tribes into four stages, viz, hunting and food gathering, pastoral, agricultural and technological. L.P. Vidyarthi & B.K. Rai, *The Tribal Culture of India...*, 96. Before the Rajputs' rule, the Bhil tribes of the southern part of Rajasthan were basically a tribe of food gatherers, hunters and fish catchers. Under the Rajputs, the Bhils started cultivating the land in the forest by slashing or burning a particular area which is communally called *Dajia* or *Jhimto*. According to the Dhebar Commission Report, the Bhils in the later part of the nineteenth century, gradually turned to cultivation. Mukul Chakraborti & Dipak Mukherji, *Indian Tribes* (Calcutta: Saraswat Library, 1971), 98. Later the non-tribal who resided in the Bhil land introduced the system of plough agriculture, which was adopted by the Bhils too. Singh, *Tribal Society in India*, 53. Mann says that the introduction of settled agriculture made a significant change in the Bhil society. R. S. Mann, "Bhil Economy and Its Problems," in *Rajasthan Bhils*, edited by N. N. Vyas R. S. Mann & N. D. Choudhary (Udaipur: Manikyalal Verma Tribal Research and Training Institute, 1978), 69.

Bhil women play a dominant role, as they are more skillful and hard working. While writing about the ST of India, Shiv Kumar Tivari comments that tribal women contribute more than men in the family. Tribal women are also seen as more careful and hard working in the field of agriculture.[67]

Reasons for Economic Backwardness

The economic institutions and their importance gradually became more prominent and started to affect the various aspects of Bhil life. The introduction of money economy, the limitations of Bhil rights in land and forest, the primitive methods of cultivation, natural calamities and harassment of sellers, traders, landlords, etc., resulted in many of the economic problems in the Bhil society.

Droughts and Famines

The state of Rajasthan regularly witnessed droughts and famines. From the 18th century onwards, the monsoon in Rajasthan has been irregular and the droughts of 1746, 1755, 1783-85, 1803-04, 1812-13, 1868-69 and 1899 turned the region into a rocky desert. Little assistance was available to the Bhils, while in regions directly administered by the British, people received some assistance. The Bhils of Kherwara taluks of Udaipur district had to survive on wild root onions, even the touching of which causes itching, especially during the six months off-season.[68]

In 1889-90, the whole of the region was under the grip of a most severe famine, still remembered as *Chhapaniya Kal*, which was popularly known as the 'famine of the fifty six' (after the Vikram Samvat year of 1956). The Bhils became

---

[67] The 1971 Census shows that all over India, 11.85% of non-tribal women were active whereas 20.7% of the tribal women were active. Jagadish Chandra Meena, *Bheel Janjathi Ka Sanskritik Eyom Arthik Jhevan (1858-1947)* (Hindi) [Social and Economic Life of Bhil Scheduled Tribe] (Udaipur: Himanshu Publications, 2003), 51.

[68] Ahuja, *Folklore of Rajasthan...*, 17-18.

desperate and many left their homes and went to Ahmedabad and Bombay to serve as labourers.[69] This was followed by another cholera epidemic, which took a heavy toll on life. As a result, the population of Kherwara decimated and it has been reported that 5 per cent of the inhabitants died of cholera within a fortnight.[70] Erskine further mentions that most of the dead were the Bhils, who had come in search of work at the site of relief works.[71] In 1950, the Bhil-dominated places in the Udaipur district were declared as famine-stricken areas.[72]

Bonded labour (*Hali*)

Kosambi and other historians relate the rise of bonded labour[73] with the periods of famine, during which tribals became enmeshed in a debt relationship from which neither they nor the following generation could escape.[74] The 1868 famine was followed by a cholera epidemic, which made the Bhils, who being economically the weakest, the worst hit. G. H. Ojha writes that "finding the local administration totally incapable of redeeming the situation, the British Government allowed the purchase of slaves and the Bhil children were sold even for two rupees each."[75]

---

[69]Erskine, *Rajputhana Gazetteers…*, 79.

[70] "Udaipur State," in *The Imperial Gazetteer of India* (Oxford: The Clarendon Press, 1908), 98.

[71]Erskine, *Rajputhana Gazetteers…*, 79.

[72] Cherian, "Contribution of the Churches…, 17.

[73] The system of *hali* was not only prevalent in southern Rajasthan, but also in western India. In some cases, several generations were forced to accept the bondage of the money-lenders, which is known as the *sagri* system in Rajasthan. Trivedi, *Towards Social Mobility…*, 38. The hali system has been abolished by The Bonded Labour System (Abolition) Act, 1976. Mathur, *Resistance Movement…*, 18.

[74] D. D. Kosambi, *An Introduction of the Study of Indian History* (Bombay: Popular Press, 1956), 353.

[75] G. H. Ojha, *The History of Rajputana* vol.3, Ajmer: 1936, 1108. Cited by N.N. Vyas, *Bondage and Exploitation in Tribal India* (Jaipur: Rawat Publications, 1980), 90.

Forced Labour (*Begar* System)

In addition to the poor economy, many Bhils were subjected to *begar* and Hindu rulers occasionally levied taxes on them. P. C. Jain comments that in the history of Rajasthan, even women, young or old, married or widowed, were not exempted from this kind of labour. Women were required to do free service inside the apartments (*Raniwas* or *Rawla*) of landlords.[76]

This kind of life was characterised by a lack of means of livelihood, chronic destitution and criminal neglect of their needs and requirements by the administration, forcing the Bhils to a criminal career.[77]

Peripatetic Traders

Under the influence of the British rule, penetration of outsiders from the plains, such as revenue officials, moneylenders, contractors, *kalals* (liquor contractors), traders and shopkeepers, caused major economic unrest among the Bhils.[78] When currency was introduced in Rajasthan, the Bhils were cheated and were paid less.[79] While writing about Jabhua (Madhya Pradesh), Buchanan comments that the Bhils were exploited even while they were dying in the great

---

[76] P. C. Jain, *Tribal Agrarian Movement* (Udaipur: Himanshu Publications, 1989), 42. In 1941, *Beggar* was abolished. Hira Singh, *Colonial Hegemony and Popular Resistance: Princes, Peasants, and Paramount Power* (New Delhi: Sage Publications, 1998), 172.

[77] Majumdar, *Races and Culture...*, 377. In order to escape from starvation during famine, some Bhils took recourses to robbery and stealing while others collected *bolai* and *rakhwali* . Bolai was taken from travelers passing through the Bhil area in return for safe and secure transit of men and goods. Rakhwali was paid by villagers of the plain to the Bhils for paying vigil and watch for their resources. Mathur, *Resistance Movement...*, 17.

[78] Sharma, *Tribal Revolts...*, 41-42.

[79] Money as a store and measurement of value and medium of exchange was not used widely among the Bhils but instruments like banking and credit are used only in dealing with non-tribal groups, which depends upon the nature and frequency of contacts with them. L.P. Vidyarthi & B.K. Rai, *The Tribal Culture of India...*, 98.

famine of 1900-01. Corn bought from the poor Bhils at a low price was sold at a profit of 900 per cent.[80]

Illiteracy

Shakra Bhai underlines that "in Kherwara there were middle school for high caste but Bhil children were not allowed. It has been said that Thakurs (local rulers) had the order from the Maharana of Udaipur not to educate the Bhils, as they were regarded equal to harijans (untouchables)."[81] The general opinion was that the Bhils would never study. He further says that "missionaries brought us the light of education but we were afraid to go to school as Thakurs used to punish those children who went to school." Once a Bhil boy of Ranjapur village was asked to stop going to school but when he persisted, a big stone was placed on his back so that he may not rise up.[82] The economic dependence of the Bhils on landlords and merchants also resulted in their lack of education.

SOCIO-RELIGIOUS AND POLITICAL REFORM MOVEMENTS

The Bhil society can be seen as a segmentary tribe, as they are bound by the norms of clan and the territory of their village. Goyal argues that "no systematic movement, however, of any kind started among the Bhils for their social development."[83] But it can be noted that several efforts had been taken both officially and unofficially for the upliftment of the Bhils; for example, the establishment of Mewar Bhil Corps (MBC) in 1840 by the British administration.

---

[80] John Buchanan, *Jungle Tales* (Toronto: The Thorn Press, 1938), 74.

[81] Interview with Shakra Bhai Daniel Bhai Hahari, Retired Headmaster, Masaro-ke-Obri, Kherwara, 18 April 2009.

[82] Interview with Shakra Bhai Daniel Bhai...

[83] Goyal, "Community Development..., 35.

As a result of the continuous interaction between the socio-religious movements (known as Messianic Movements), the Bhil society has undergone a transition in its socio-cultural life. They have been influenced by Islam, Hinduism and Christianity. But Christian missionaries and the Bhagat cult of Hinduism had a greater influence on the tribals in Rajasthan.[84]

Mewar Bhil Corps (MBC)

In 1818, the Bhils came within the sphere of British influence and the British wanted to adopt some method to stop them from daily dacoities and petty warfare, which disturbed the neighboring rulers and territories. So in 1825 a British officer, Lt. Gen. Sir James Outram (1803-1863), who was one of the most sympathetic soldiers to serve India, was sent to 'tame the Bhils.' He was able to bring the Bhils of the hilly tracts in central India and Khandesh into order during the years 1828-38.[85]

With a similar objective, the British government started the MBC in 1840 and raised several regiments of Bhil soldiers with a view of preserving peace in the remote and troublesome tribal areas with its headquarters in Kherwara (Udaipur).[86] The main purpose of the MBC was to check the tribal uprisings and to bring about a change in the traditional

---

[84] Doshi says that the Mohammedans as carriers of culture had no impact on the way of living of the Bhils. Mainly because the Sunni Muslims who were the members of the police department of the state acted as agents of oppression against the Bhils. It was through them that they were terrorized to submit to the royal orders. But, on the other hand, the Boharas (Shia Muslim), who were petty traders, partially influenced the Bhil style of life like change in spoken dialect and drinking of tea. Doshi, *Bhils: Between Societal...*, 20.

[85] Outram in Khandesh, first gained the Bhils confidence and then formed his Bhil friends into armed police to keep their fellow Bhils in order. Eyre Chatterton, *India through a Bishop's Diary* (London: SPCK, 1935), 78.

[86] The Corps had stations at Kherwara, Mt. Abu and Kota (in Rajasthan). R.H.S. Boyd, *A Church History of Gujarat* (Madras: The Christian Literature Society, 1981), 63.

life of the people. Actually, the objective of the corps (1860-64) was to wean "a semi savage race (Bhils) from its predatory habits giving them honorable employment and assisting the Mewar State in preserving order."[87] Thus MBC made tremendous inroads into the tribal way of life, which made the Bhils abide by the law and provided them with employment opportunities with the hope of giving them a respectable status parallel to their heroic life.

Impact of MBC

The Bhils were recruited in MBC with the motto of maintaining peace and harmony in the Bhil land. They got their first great recognition of being trustworthy and capable of living a disciplined life. MBC officials provided education and medical facilities for Bhil soldiers. A few of them had social upliftment but because of the Bhils' independent nature, they were not bound to obey anyone's rule and till the late 19th century, they lived according to their old values, carrying on their internal feuds, raiding and looting villages outside their own *pals* and persecuting alleged witches.[88]

Messianic Movements

The messianic movements[89] were started among the Bhils in the last decade of the 19th century and the early part of the 20th century. It had a profound impact on the Bhil way of life. These movements, which were led by men claiming supernatural powers, were a reaction to the oppression and expropriation of tribal populations by economically and

---

[87] Doshi, "The Changing Patterns…, 137.

[88] Hardiman, *Missionaries…*, 241.

[89] L.P. Mathur classifies Messianic Movement as Social Movement and defines it as "participation of a divine saviour in human flesh in the trans-formation of the mazeway." Mazeway is again defined as an individual's mental image of total society and culture. L.P. Mathur, *Movements of Tribals during the Colonial Rule: Role of Ideologies* (New Delhi: Inter-India Publications, 1995), 15.

politically more powerful groups.[90] These movements though religious in nature were essentially social and cultural movements in outcome. It was stressed that the fight of the Bhils was against the rulers who had driven them to the forest, but this struggle could not be successful unless the Bhils acquired inner strength through the adoption of the puritanical and ritualistic Hindu rules and restrictions of life. This basic concept of the messianic movement resulted in the partial Hinduisation of the Bhils.[91]

The Mavji-Guru-na-bhagat Movement

Mavji[92] is believed to have lived nearly three centuries ago. He seems to be a mythical leader and his movement is known as the oldest Bhagat movement among the Bhils. In the nineteenth century, it was revived as a Vaishnavite movement, which made a great impact among the Bhils of south Rajasthan, especially in the areas of Banswara, Udaipur and Dungarpur. The main teachings of Mavji were introduction of vegetarianism, rejection of *dapa* (bride price) and wearing of *bana* (cotton thread) on the neck and putting of a vaishnavite sectarian mark on the forehead.[93]

The Lusadiya Movement

The Lusadiya movement[94] was started in the last decade of the 19th century, around 1860s, by a Bhil of Lusadiya named

---

[90] Christoph von Furer-Haimendorf, "Traditional Leadership in Indian Tribal Societies," in *Leadership in South Asia*, edited by B.N. Pandey (Delhi: Vikas Publishing House, 1977), 16.

[91] Stephan Fuchs, *Rebellious Prophets: A Study of Messianic Movements in Indian Religions* (Bombay: Asia Publishing House, 1965), 239-240.

[92] According to Mann, Mavji was considered as the tenth incarnation of Vishnu and was born in a Gaur Brahmin family of Sabla village in Dungarpur District. Along with the worship of the trinity of Brahma, Vishnu and Mahesh, the Mavjis also instructed the Bhils about their social, spiritual and economic upliftment. Mann, "Structure and Role Dynamics...., 315.

[93] *Ibid.*, 315-316.

[94] Stephan Fuchs describes this movement as Lasodia Movement. Fuchs, *Rebellious Prophets...*, 239-240.

Surmal Das. He proclaimed that he possessed divine power and he performed miracles for the emancipation of the tribe. He advised his followers to lead a righteous and virtuous life. Deception, theft, adultery and rape should never be committed by the members of this movement and all kinds of meat and alcoholic drinks were forbidden. Surmal Das declared that all traditional practices of witchcraft and magic should be abolished and God Rama alone should be worshipped.[95]

The Govindgiri and Bhagat Movement

R. S. Mann states that Govindgiri,[96] started a movement around 1911, reasserted the teachings of his former leaders like Mavji Guru. He encouraged the Bhils to create a new society by worshiping Rama and leading a good moral life.[97] His reforms were greatly influenced by the Vaishnavite and Shaivite schools of thought. Through all these processes, as M. N. Srinivas and Syam Lal argue, the basic intention behind Govindgiri was to sanskritise the Bhils and to bring them to the level of others in the Hindu caste society.[98]

Govindgiri called his followers Bhagats and they enjoined to be teetotalers and vegetarians.[99] It attracted the Bhils

---

[95] *Ibid.*

[96] Govindgiri, was a Banjara by caste. He was a disciple of a Gosain-Hindu monk named Rajgiri. Govindgiri's association with Swami Dayanand gave him a vision to do something better for the Bhil community. He declared that he was an incarnation of god and that it was his mission to reform the degenerate Bhils. Jain, *Christianity, Ideology...,* 155.

[97] He also forbade inter-dining with outsiders, even with Brahmins, and pollution. He asked his followers to always speak the truth, not to steal, nor to lust for another man's wife, abstain from meat and wine. P.C. Jain stated that the attack on meat consumption was primarily governed by Jain and Brahminical influences. *Ibid.,* 155-56.

[98] *Ibid.,* 161. He was also much influenced by the doctrine of Shudhi proposed by Dayanand Saraswati, the founder of the Arya Samaj. Hardiman, "Assertion, Conversion...,* 256.

[99] S.L. Doshi, *The Changing Bhils in Banswara: A Study in Bhil Acculturation,* vol. 6 (Udaipur: The University of Rajasthan Studies, 1960), 144.

because of its merits like better status and recognition in the Bhil society. According to S. K. Navlakha, "[t]he basic principles which guide a Bhagat's conduct are devotion, non-violence and truth, each of which involves a number of formal and conventional observances."[100]

Govindgiri also initiated political reforms by establishing a Bhil Kingdom of which he would be the head.[101] However, he was subdued by the ruler of Banswara with the help of the MBC and British Artillery. This was a major setback for the whole movement.[102]

Impact of Bhagatism

To some extent, Bhagatism transformed and gave social recognition to the Bhils; as a result of which, they gave up their traditional religious practice and magical values. Traditional deities were replaced by Hindu gods and the religious elements included daily prayers, worship of deity, practice of monogamy and so on.[103] The fieldwork done by Avlakha describes the impact of Bhagatism on the Bhil society as follows:

> The Bhagat Bhils occupy the uppermost status…The Bhagat Bhils would not accept water at the hands of ordinary Bhils unless it is contained and fetched in a metallic (copper or brass) vessel….. Both food and water are, however, unconditionally refused by the Bhagat Bhils at the hands of the Christian Bhils.[104]

---

[100] Jain, *Christianity, Ideology…*, 158. But the Bhagat Bhils did not adhere to the ways of non-violence. For instance, in December 1921, Govindgiri along with a large number of Bhils beat up three revenue officials in the Jhalore (Mewar) while they were collecting revenue. Similar acts of violence took place in the surrounding areas. C. S. K. Singh, "Bhils' Participation in Politics in Rajasthan in the 1920's," *Social Scientist* 13/4 (April, 1985). http://www.jstor.org/stable/3517516 [1 Feb 2010]. 34.

[101] Mann, "Structure and Role…, 316.

[102] In the year 1911, Govindgiri summoned a meeting on the Mangarh hill of Banswara. A large number of the Bhils from Banswara, Udaipur, Dungarpur and Bhils from Gujarat also attended this meeting. Roop Singh, "Anatomy of Three Tribal Movements in Rajasthan," *Eastern Anthropologist* 36/2 (April-June, 1983): 122.

[103] Jain, *Christianity, Ideology…*, 169.

[104] *Ibid.*, 161, 162.

In south Rajasthan, it is reported that the Bhagat Bhils withdrew their children from a school in the Gudawat village of Kherwara (Udaipur), as there were no separate drinking pots for the children of Bhagat Bhils.[105] R. S. Mann says "…the Bhagat rarely participate in the traditional functions of the non-Bhagat."[106] The movement is now purely puritanical in nature and is restricted largely to social life.

Summary

The Bhils had their own egalitarian governing systems, religious customs and practices. They have their own worldview of life and religion. The socio-religious and political movements among the Bhils to an extent resulted in social transformation and integration of several religious and cultural characteristics that were not found in them traditionally. In spite of the impact of such influences, they still maintain their distinctiveness and uniqueness as a tribe in Rajasthan.

---

[105] R. S. Mann, "Bhils and Culture Contact-Case of Social Grouping," in *Rajasthan Bhils*, edited by R. S. Mann & N. D. Choudhary N. N. Vyas (Udaipur: Manikyalal Verma Tribal Research and Training Institute, 1978), 66.

[106] Mann, "Structure and Role…, 321.

Chapter 3

AN ANALYSIS OF CHRISTIAN MISSION AMONG THE BHIL TRIBE

Christianity made its entry into Rajasthan in the late 18th century. Initially, the Bhils were suspicious of Christian mission, as it was always considered to be a part of the colonial rule. Soon this concept changed and many started accepting the Christian faith. Shyam Lal says that in Rajasthan, the Bhil community was the largest responsive race to the Christian faith.[1] But often a majority of historical writers have seen this growth as a result of missionaries' proselytisation,[2] which resulted in natural unrest among the tribals, made poor tribal, poor converts,[3] destroyed the culture of the Bhils and divided them. The Niyogi Commission Report of 1956 also argues on the same line based on some empirical data and findings.

The first half of this chapter focuses on Christian missions, mainly the CMS mission, among the Bhils in Kherwara, Udaipur. The second half deals with an analysis of the missionary activities with the arguments made by the Niyogi Report and others. This chapter also enquires whether the missionary work caused divisions among the Bhils. What kinds of inducements were used for converting the Bhils in Kherwara, Udaipur? What was the role played, if any, by the Christian Mission to uplift the Bhil tribe? Did the converts deny their tribal identify?

---

[1] Lal, *Tribals and Christian…*, 15.

[2] S. S. Shashi, ed., *Encyclopaedia of Indian Tribes*, Vol. 1: The Tribal World in Transition (New Delhi: Anmol Publications, 1994), 44. S. R. Toppo, *Tribes in India* (Delhi: Indian Publishers Distributors, 2000), 189,199.

[3] Shashi, ed., *Encyclopaedia …*, 4.

CHRISTIAN MISSIONS

The story of the origin and growth of the church among the Bhils of Rajasthan is of great importance, as it helps to understand the role of mission and its social and cultural impact on their life. Four important mission agencies came to Rajasthan between 1880 and 1954, viz. the Scottish Presbyterians in 1876, CMS in 1880, the Canadian Presbyterians in 1913 and Roman Catholic mission by 1921.[4] A detailed study is done only by the CMS mission, as it was the only main mission among the Bhils of Kherwara, Udaipur, from 1880 to 1954. This is also an attempt to understand how they worked among the Bhils and what their role was in general among the Bhils of Rajasthan.

THE SCOTTISH PRESBYTERIAN MISSION

Dr. James Shepherd (1847-1929) was appointed a missionary of the United Presbyterian Church to Rajputana in November 1877.[5]   During his first visit itself, he was much impressed by the Bhils of Kherwara, Udaipur, when Colonel Gordon, the then commandant of the MBC in Kherwara station, helped them to meet the headmen of the Bhils who gave the permission to speak to his people.[6]

Shepherd based his ministry in Udaipur city, but he was always fascinated by the Bhils who came down the mountains to the city with grass and wood to sell. His heart was

---

[4] There were other missions also working among the Bhils in the surrounding areas like the United Free Church Mission north from Udaipur; the Irish Presbyterian Mission on the south from Godhra and Dohad; and the Canadian Presbyterian Mission on the south-east from Ratlam (M.P.). *Handbook for Workers: Outline Histories of the C.M.S. Missions*, vol. 2 (London: Church Missionary Society, 1906), 94.

[5] Dr. James Shepherd was born in Aberdeen, Scotland. William F. Martin, *Martin Memorials: Life and Work of William and Gavin Martin* (Edinburgh: Her Majesty's Stationary Office, 1886), 271-72; Ewing Smith, "Mission in Rajasthan," *Pilgrim* no. 35 (August 2009): 19. Jacob K. Jacob, "The Shepherd of Udaipur," *Cross & Crown* 26/1 (October/November, 1995): 2.

[6] Martin, *Martin Memorials…*, 275.

completely dedicated to the Bhils so, along with his catechist Isa Das, he used to go into the territories where the Bhils lived to help them medically and to disseminate the basic knowledge of cleanliness and the methods of maintaining proper hygiene. Because of the love and care of Shepherd a long-lasting relationship had been established between the mission and the Bhils.[7] The headmen of the villages entrusted their sons to his care, and the Bhil Boys' Home was founded in July 1883.[8] But in 1899, because of famine, the Bhil Home was turned into an orphanage, with at a time three hundred inmates.[9]

Shepherd served the community with his medical skills and the people appreciated his service, as he was willing to treat all without any barriers.[10] Both the people and the State authorities greatly appreciated Shepherd service and he was also honoured twice with the *Kaiser-e-Hind* medal for his sacrificial love and care for the people of the country.[11]

He worked in Udaipur for almost 40 years, but due to ill health on 19th June 1920, he left Udaipur never to return and he died on 29th March 1926.[12] By this time, CMS missionaries had made permanent settlements in the Bhil land of Udaipur, i.e., Kherwara. The Scottish Presbyterian Mission thereafter concentrated only in the city of Udaipur.

---

[7] George Carstairs, *The Shepherd of Udaipur and the Land He Loved* (London: Hodder & Stoughton, 1926), 240.

[8] Jacob K. Jacob, "The Shepherd of Udaipur," *Cross & Crown* 26/1 (October/November, 1995): 2.Jacob, "The Shepherd…, 7. By 1888 there were 27 boys on the roll, and this was about the average in the years that followed. Ashcroft, "Story of Our Rajputana…, 76.

[9] Carstairs, *The Shepherd…*, 250.

[10] Frank Ashcroft, "Story of Our Rajputana Mission," in *United Free Church of Scotland: Mission in India*, edited by United Free Church of Scotland (Edinburgh: United Free Church of Scotland, 1909), 74.

[11] Frank Ashcroft, "Story of Our Rajputana Mission…, 74. The medal was instituted by Queen Victoria on April 10, 1900. The name translates as "Emperor of India", a name also used for a rare Indian butterfly *Teinopalpus imperialis*. The Kaiser-e-Hind ceased to be awarded following the Indian Independence, 1947.

[12] Jacob, "The Shepherd…, 7.

CHURCH MISSIONARY SOCIETY

In 1877, at CMS headquarters in London, a conference was held on the theme 'Non-Aryan Missions.' The conference concluded that the hill-tribes of India 'would soon be Hinduized if Christians did not step in.' As a direct outcome of the meeting, H. D. Williamson was sent to Mandla, Madhya Pradesh, to establish a CMS Gond mission in the Central Provinces; and in 1878, two new stations, Barharwa and Bhagaya, were opened in the Santal Parganas in western Bengal. Two years later, C. S. Thompson was sent as a pioneer missionary to the Bhils at Kherwara on the western border of Rajputana.[13]

BHIL MISSION

The CMS Bhil Mission[14] included the border territories of Kherwara in Rajasthan and Lusadiya and Bhiladia, presently

---

[13] This conference was attended by several eminent former administrators in India, such as Sir William Muir and Sir George Yule, and pioneer missionaries, such as E.L. Puxley, W.T. Storrs and E. Champion, who were already working among the Santals and Gonds in India. Gordon Hewitt, *The Problem of Success: A History of the Church Missionary Society 1910-1942*, vol. 2, Asia (Great Britain: Overseas Partners, 1977), 114.

[14] Bhil Mission came under the administration of different CMS Diocese as it had only few centres in North India. First, it was the part of the Calcutta Diocese and the mission was under the care of the Metropolitan of India. Eyre Chatterton, *A History of the Church of England in India: Since the Early Days of the East India Company* (London: SPCK, 1924), 216.When the Lucknow Diocese was formed, it came under the care of the Allahabad Corresponding Committee and in 1903, when Nagpur diocese was carved out, the Bhil mission came under the Jabbulpore (Jabalpur) Corresponding Committee. It was in 1915, with the formation of Bombay Diocese, as it was nearer to Kherwara, the Bhil Mission was transferred to them and finally in April 1915, it came under the CMS diocese of Western India Mission. The main reasons were the nearness of the new mission with the Bhil territory. Jabalpur was about 400 miles from the Bhil Mission and Bombay was much nearer and in other ways more satisfactory as the mission headquarters, and the Gujarati language, which is spoken in the Bhil Mission area, is widely spoken in the Bombay Diocese, (but nowhere else in Nagpur Diocese). On these grounds, the CMS missionaries requested the transfer, which was finally granted. "Central Provinces and Rajputana," in *Proceedings of the Church Missionary Society for Africa and the East 1915-16* (London: Church Missionary House, 1916), 115. Hewitt, *The Problem of Success...*, 120.

in Gujarat. [15] Kherwara became the centre of CMS with the help of MBC officials.[16] Among the British Officers was Capt. Rundall, Adjutant of the Mewar Bhil Corps, who married Rosa Bickersteth (known as the patron saint of Kherwara), daughter of Rev. E. H. Bickersteth of Hampstead.[17] Mrs. Rosa Rundall, through letters, conveyed to her father the degraded condition of the poor Bhils around Kherwara[18] which in turned resulted in his offer of 1,000 Pounds to the CMS to send their missionary to the Bhils. As a result, Rev. C. S. Thompson arrived in Kherwara on 27 November 1880. Before he arrived, the All Saints' Church had been built on 29th September 1878 as a worship place for the officials of MBC.[19]

FIRST MISSIONARY: CHARLES STEWART THOMPSON

Rev. C. S. Thompson came to India from Earington in Durham on 27 November 1880. He received a warm welcome from Dr. James Shepherd, who took him on a tour to acquaint him with the Bhil land and learn the language.

Initially, the Bhils did not trust Thompson, as they doubted him for two things. They thought that he had come

---

[15] In pre-Independent India, the territories were divided based on Linguistic association and on ethnicity or cultural ties. Robert W. Stern, *Changing India: Bourgeois Revolution on the Subcontinent* (New Delhi: Cambridge University Press, 1998), 105.

[16] Jacob K. Jacob, "The Grain of Wheat in the Bhil Land: Rev. Charles Stewart Thompson," *Cross & Crown* 27/3 (March-April, 1997): 2.

[17] Bickersteth was later also ordained as the Bishop of Exeter. Eugene Stock, *The History of the Church Missionary Society: Its Environment, Its Men and Its Work*, vol. III (London: Church Missionary Society, 1899), 262.

[18] Mrs. Rundall wrote to her father that the visits of their clergyman, the government chaplain of Neemuch, Central India, was very infrequent so arrangement should be made for some permanent resident priest in Kherwara. Chatterton, *India...*, 78.

[19] The church was built in memory of Baby Theodore, Mrs. Rundalls' son, and dedicated by the Bishop of Calcutta (Edward Ralph Johnson) in 1878. The church played an important role among the officials of Mewar Bhil Corps, as there were no other within a 100 miles. "Rajputana Mission," in *Proceedings of the Church Missionary Society for Africa and the East 1880-81* (London: Church Missionary House, 1881), 83.

to kill them or to levy fresh taxes on them, and the Census taken in the very year he arrived added to their fears.[20] Thompson writes of his own difficulties in his annual report:

> Things being so, when I visited the chiefs I hardly dared to speak upon any topic whatever. If I inquired about the family, then how very naturally might they have looked upon me as another enumerator. If I spoke about the cattle, fields, or crops, then the tax question might have disturbed their minds. To talk about God, I knew that with them, as with others, nothing could so readily or so strongly call forth their highest fears. There was, moreover, another obstacle to be overcome…. I had hoped to have relieved sufferers, and to have gained a hearing by treating their sick. I found, however, that they were full of fear on this head also.[21]

However, later, his knowledge of medicine enabled him to overcome their fears.[22] He went from village to village spending almost a week in each place. Patients coming for treatment would also stay back to listen to the Gospel.[23] Thompson felt the great need of patience and he started focusing separately on three main strategies in order to reach the Bhils, i.e., through medicine, education and evangelism. By adopting these strategies, Thompson wanted to avoid any direct confrontation with the religious beliefs of the Bhils, whether they were of the old or reformed persuasions.[24]

---

[20] Thompson writes that the Bhils were not able to understand why the Indian census was taken. Some thought that the Queen of England was taking an account of their number, and the number of their cattle, in order to kill them all. Others thought that it was to impose fresh taxes. But others, getting still wider of the mark, said that a scheme was being prepared for giving the fat women to the fat men, and the lean women to the lean men. Stock, *The History…*, vol. 3, 196.

[21] "Central Provinces & Etc.," in *Proceedings of the Church Missionary Society for Africa and the East 1881-82* (London: Church Missionary House, 1882), 91-92.

[22] Thompson also had some medical training though he was not a qualified doctor.

[23] Jacob, "The Grain of Wheat…, 3.

[24] Hardiman, *Missionaries …*, 67.

Thompson is still remembered for his contributions and life-giving sacrifice during the famine of 1899, which is recorded as the greatest in the history of Mewar. When the famine started, he was under treatment in a nursing home in England, but hearing the need and suffering of the Bhils, he determined against strong medical advice and returned to Kherwara in early December 1899.[25] As soon as he arrived, he toured the outstations and found himself surrounded by hungry children and adults. As the native states did not help, Thompson initiated temporary houses and relief kitchens were started to feed thousands of Bhils. Special attention was given to those who were sick.[26]

During this time, cholera also broke out, and Thompson had to go to Bavalia, an outstation twenty miles away from Kherwara, to attend the patients where he himself became the victim of cholera. Soon he was carried to Kherwara with the hope of obtaining medical relief, but passed away at Zanzri, a village 3 miles from Kherwara, on 19th May 1900.[27]

Thompson is called 'the Father of the Bhils.' There is no written biography about him but his history is passed on from generation to generation through oral tradition in the *lokagita* (folk song), which is sung by Christians and non-Christians on occasions like festivals, social gatherings and marriages and during the cultural dance called *garba*.[28]

Thompson had provided the Christian church with translations of the Catechism on the nature of God, the life

---

[25] Chatterton, *A History* ..., 216.

[26] Jacob, "The Grain of Wheat..., 3.

[27] At Zanzri itself, a grave was dug and Thompson's body was laid to rest. The spot is now marked by a marble cross and tomb. Jacob, "The Grain of Wheat..., 4. Eugene Stock, *The History of the Church Missionary Society: Its Environment, Its Men and Its Work,* vol. 4 (London: Church Missionary Society, 1916), 221.

[28] Jacob, *The Grain of Wheat...,* 4. Crist Geet, CNI Som-Sabarkantha ke Mandali key Liye (Hindi), 2005, 108.

of Christ and the way of salvation, along with parts of the prayer book. He compiled Bhili folk songs, a Bhili-English grammar and vocabulary of the dialect spoken by the Bhils of Rajputana in 1895. He also prepared a historical sketch of Bhil Hillman entitled *Mahikantha*.[29]

ESTABLISHMENT AND EXPANSION OF MISSION

Kherwara

In 1883, land was bought in Kherwara and the foundation of Kherwara Mission House was laid in 1884. In Kherwara and its villages, eleven schools were opened, including one girls' school. Thompson's aim was to win children for Christ and to free them from superstition and ignorance, which was very difficult.[30] He established a mission dispensary in Kherwara for those who came from villages. He avoided treating town people as there were already three MBC doctors for them.[31] He used to take more time to visit the neighbouring Bhil villages where no medical work was available.[32] It was only on December 15, 1889, after nine

---

[29] Thompson published a primer on the Bhil Language with vocabulary and other common words prevalent among them. C.S. Thompson, *Rudiments of the Bhili Language* (Ahmedabad: Union Printing Press, 1895), 200. Sakra Bhai commonly known among the Bhils of Udaipur as Sakra master was the first Bhil graduate who later became the first B.Ed. Teacher from Masaro-ki-Obri village of Kherwara, Udaipur. Sakra Bhai Daniel Bhai Hahari, "Som Sabhar Khata Christi Adivasivo" (Gujarati) [Tribal Christians of Saum Sabhar Kata]" (B.A. thesis, Gujarat Vidhya Pheet, 1962), 9. "Central Provinces and Rajputana," in *Proceedings of the Church Missionary Society 1895-96* (London: Church Missionary House, 1896), 207. See also Hewitt, *The Problem of Success...*, 118. Only in 1917, Gospel of Mark was translated by Dr. John Buchanan of the Canadian Presbyterian Mission at Amkhut (M.P) into Bhili Dialect. J.S.M. Hooper, *Bible Translation in India, Pakistan and Ceylon* Second ed. (Bombay: Oxford University Press, 1963), 179.

[30] Jacob, "The Grain of Wheat..., 3.

[31] MBC had Charitable Dispensary, which was functioning in Kherwara before the CMS arrived. *Battling and Building...*, 51.

[32] But MBC doctors' help was always taken in case of medical emergencies. Thompson, "The Bhil Mission..., 416-417.

years, that the CMS mission got their first converts.[33] Thompson writes of the "four stages" in the story of the Bhil Mission in the following words:

> It has taken nine long years for the 'good seed' to take root, spring up, and bear fruit. There have been four clearly-marked stages in the Mission. First, 1880 to 1882, the difficulty of getting the confidence of the hillmen; second, 1883 to 1887, the convicting of sin as an offence against a Personal Holy God, and Righteous Moral Governor; third, 1888 and 1889, believing in Jesus secretly; and fourth, at the end of last year, public confession by baptism.[34]

The definite and united invitation of the people of Lusadiya and Biladiya led Thompson to open a mission station at Lusadiya, Biladiya and many other sub-stations in their villages.[35]

Lusadiya (1886)

Thomson was the first missionary in Lusadiya,[36] which is generally known as the land of Bhagats. A school was first opened in June 1887, but was closed down till the famine of 1900 because of the opposition of the Bhagats.[37] The Bhils of Lusadiya respected and obeyed all the commands of their Bhagat Guru, Surmaldas. At his death bed, he prophesied that very soon a great famine was going to come and that teachers would come and distribute free books and teach

---

[33] A 45-year-old Sukha, a Bhajat, his wife, Hirki and four children (three sons, Teza, Badha, Lalu, and daughter, Mangli) were baptised amidst much opposition on 15th December 1889. C.S. Thompson, "The Bhil Mission," in *The Church Missionary Intelligencer and Record* (London: Church Missionary House, Sep.1890), 609-10. The opposition was so strong that the eldest daughter, who was married to a Bhagat, was poisoned shortly after. *Handbook for Workers...*, 92.

[34] Stock, *The History...*, vol. 3, 468.

[35] In all mission documents, Lusadiya and Biladiya is spelled as *Lusadia* and *Biladia*.

[36] Lusadiya was situated (as the border of Mewar State), in Idar State of present Gujarat and was commonly known as *Nani Marwar* (Little Marwar). But the missionaries did not find much difference between the Bhils of Kherwara and Lusadiya. As they both spoke Gujarati and as they intermarried, they were related too. Hardiman, *Missionaries..*, 57-58.

[37] *Handbook for Workers...*, 93.

the true way of salvation, which can be attained through believing in the sinless incarnated born of a virgin.[38] After Surmaldas' demise, the famine of 1899-1900 broke out, which led many of the Bhagat disciples to compare his sayings for three days with the Bible. Finally, struck by the wonderful resemblance in many respects, they received baptism and they themselves constructed a church on the spot where the holy fire of Bhagatism was formerly kept burning.[39]

Biladiya (1888)

Missionaries started working at Biladiya[40] at the request of the chief of the village. The village chiefs were initially very cooperative, but as the Christian work progressed and the Bhils became aware of being cheated by their village leaders, the *thakurs* or the chieftain started opposing the Christian Bhil and the mission. Biladiya became the centre of extensive famine relief work during 1900, and since then became one of the main outstations of Bhil Mission.[41]

ROLE OF WOMEN MISSIONARIES

Dana L. Robert says that the notion of 'Women's work for Women' was not only instrumental in the field of education, medical work and evangelisation, but also tried to elevate the social status of women that was enjoyed in Christian countries.[42] The CMS women missionaries played great roles

---

[38] *Battling and Building...*, 26.

[39] *Handbook for Workers...*, 93. Many others also had vision like Lalu and Surji Bhai Thimodi. *Battling and Building...*, 26.

[40] Bilaria is twenty miles to the west of Kherwara.

[41] The *thakurs,* opposition was so great that they imposed more forced labour on Christian Bhils than on others. *Handbook for Workers...*, 93.

[42] Robert says that by the middle of the 19th century, the women of America became conscious of their role in evangelism so the missionary wives and single women united to form their own independent organisation for mission. She says that "Woman's work for Woman" was based on a maternalistic, albeit idealistic, belief that non-Christian religions trapped and degraded women, yet all women in the world were sisters and should support each other. Dana L. Robert, *American Women in Mission: A Social History of Their Thought and Practice* (Macon, Georgia: Mercer University Press, 1998), 125-133.

in the Bhil mission.[43] They contributed in administering hostels, giving medical care, evangelising and giving hygiene classes for the mothers of the family. Both married and single women ministered among the Bhils. Some of the women missionaries were Miss Holdom, Miss Bull, Miss Rose Carter, Mrs. Dr Jane Birkett, Mrs. Frank Read and Mrs Margaret Johnson.

They held special literacy classes for women. But initially it was not easy for them to get sufficient pupils because of the male dominant thought and ignorance of the Bhil society. Traditionally, Bhil women enjoyed greater freedom of equality than any other caste women of Rajasthan, but because of their close interaction with the Hindus, they started practicing purity and pollution. Hardiman quoting Miss. B.M. Newton says that even the Bhil converts saw little need for female education. But soon that notion changed, as they started realising the importance of female education.[44] Miss B. M. Newton further reports that the most successful work for women was carried out through the orphanage for girls, where girls stayed and received education.[45]

THE NIYOGI REPORT AND OTHERS' CRITICISM

In 1956, the Madhya Pradesh government constituted a fact-finding committee under the chairmanship of M. B. Niyogi.[46] He states that the immediate cause of this team was to look into the complaints received from the public on the

---

[43] CMS as a mission did not favour sending out single women as missionaries to India. They followed the resolution of 1867, which says that already the 'wives, sisters and daughters' of the CMS missionaries are working unpaid so no need of employing single women. But their concept was changed in 1880 and soon single missionaries were sent to work exclusively among the women of India. Stock, *The History...*, vol. 2, 398-399.

[44] Hardiman, *Missionaries...*, 142.

[45] *Ibid.*, 144.

[46] *Report of the Christian Missionary Activities Enquiry Committee Madhya Pradesh, 1956.* This report is popularly known as Niyogi Report and is published in two volumes.

objectionable activities of some mission organisations, especially in the tribal areas of Madhya Pradesh.[47] He further cites that government officials have received reports against Christian missionaries that their relationship to the State was not healthy and "their methods not savoury."[48]

On receiving this report, Niyogi and his team visited different regions where Christian Missions and Christians were numerous. They came out with ten findings about missionary activities. The report declares that a large amount of foreign currency is channeled into the country for missionary work, comprising of educational, medical and evangelical activities, which results in proselytisation. Thus Christianity is the result of "undue influence, misrepresentation, etc., or in other words not by conviction but by various inducements offered for proselytization in various forms."[49] "Schools, hospitals and orphanages are used as a means to facilitate proselytization."[50] It also stated that Christian tribals assert a sense of unity and solidarity among themselves so "there is a danger of his loyalty to his country and State."[51] Based on these finding, the Niyogi report recommended that missionaries and mission activities should be restricted and "those missionaries whose primary object is proselytization should be asked to withdraw."[52]

The Niyogi report caused great controversy and anxiety among the various Christian missions and others all around

---

[47] *Report of the Christian Missionary Activities Enquiry Committee Madhya Pradesh, 1956,* vol. 1, pp. 6, 18.

[48] *Report of the Christian Missionary* ..., 7.

[49] *Report of the Christian* Missionary..., 131.

[50] *Report of the Christian Missionary...,* 132. Niyogi contradicts his own argument as many in his own witness list testified that they did not convert based on inducement but due to different reasons, such as reading the Bible, social acceptance and because of the love of Jesus manifested through the missionaries. *Report of the Christian Missionary Activities Enquiry Committee Madhya Pradesh, 1956* vol. 2, Part B, pp. 73, 103, 105, 192, 193, 195, 197, 214, 215, 234 and 279.

[51] *Report of the Christian Missionary* ..., vol.1, 131.

[52] *Report of the Christian Missionary...,* 392-94.

India. Though the recommendations of the Niyogi Report were not implemented, it is important to study it as it reflected the general attitude of a number of people in India.[53]

Niyogi's accusation against Christian mission is relevant here, as the same accusations were leveled against the Bhil Mission of Rajasthan. The missionaries were blamed for taking the support of foreign officials and for using all means available for proselytisation. H. S. Srivastava says that a large number of orphans were eventually converted to Christianity during the famine year both directly and with the government's help.[54] R. S. Mann argues that the approach of Christian missionaries involved material benefits, which the convert Bhils could get. This attraction encouraged and gave way to the process of proselytisation. The converts are also bent upon declaring themselves as an endogamous group, and at times, deny their tribal identity.[55]

Based on this argument, let us look at the Bhil Mission in Kherwara, Udaipur.

MISSIONARY METHODS AND ACTIVITIES OF THE BHIL CHURCH

Hardiman writes that the Bhils were never the passive objects of missionary attention and that the missionaries had to constantly adapt and modify their strategies to gain a response from them.[56] They were actively involved in the

---

[53] M.K. Kuriakose, *History of Christianity in India: Source Materials* (Madras: The Christian Literature Society, 1982), 390. Surajit Sinha highlighting the impact of Christianity says that conversion of tribals led to their being uprooted from their traditional norm. Surajit Sinha, "Tribes and Indian Civilization: Transformation Processes in Morden India," *Man in India* 61/2 (June, 1981): 111.

[54] Srivastava, "Dimensions…, 224.

[55] Mann, "Bhils and Culture…, 63.

[56] Thompson, the first missionary, arrived in Kherwara believing that the Bhils were a kind of tabula rasa on which missionaries might write with ease. He thought that when they are exposed to the truth of the gospel, the Bhils, like other primitive tribes, would quickly accept its message. But he soon understood that they were not the way he thought, so he used his medical knowledge to reach their body first than their soul, which turned to be a great acceptable practice in the mission. Hardiman, *Missionaries…*, 19, 57.

social upliftment of the Bhil community through their different projects of education and medical and relief work, which propelled the Bhils towards holistic development.

In the Bhil Mission of Kherwara, the growth of Christianity was not rapid, but gradual in nature and the conversions of Bhils were not based on inducements; they were based on self-conviction. It took almost eleven years for the Bhil mission to get its first convert.

General Evangelistic Approach

Missionaries made Kherwara their base and from there they used to go to the interior village and live among the Bhils in tents usually for two to three weeks. They had the working knowledge of Hindi and Guajarati other than Bhili or Vagiri, which helped them to communicate the gospel.[57] As the Bhils lived in scattered houses and assembled only during marriages or funeral services,[58] missionaries and local Christians used those opportunities to preach the word of God. Missionaries also used Lantern Slides and film shows as means of evangelism and of spreading medical awareness.[59]

Church Planting

The missionaries in the Bhil land saw the Bhil congregation as a Bhil church. In 1889, after receiving the first baptised family, Thompson declared in his report that "you now

---

[57] "Rajputana Mission," Proceedings…, 1880-81, 83.

[58] "West India Mission," in *Proceedings of the Church Missionary Society for Africa and the East 1918-1919* (London: Church Missionary House, 1919), 78. C.L. Shaw, "Kherwara, Rajputana", in Report of the CMS Western India Mission, 1918, 54.

[59] Illustrated scenes from the Bible were projected and it was also used for medical awareness. E.P. Herbert, Kherwara, North-West Provinces', CMS: Extracts from the Annual Letters of the Missionaries, 1896, 140; Lanterns were commonly known among the Bhils as magic lantern (*Jadui Fhanas*). Daniel Kala Sua, History of CMS in Bhil Land (Hindi), unpublished handwritten Manuscript, n.d., 5. By 1954, the missionaries organised film shows. The Rev. R. G. Bhanat Writes, Bhil Mission Report, 1954, 9 and The Ven. P. H. Johnson Writes, Bhil Mission Report, 1954, 17.

have a Bhil Christian Church."[60] In 1912, Birkett challenged the methods illustrated by Roland Allen and argued that "the Bhil Church worked on exceptionally simple lines."[61] They followed the general principle of CMS mission proliferated by Henry Venn's principles of self-support, self-governance and self-extending in developing the independent native Church.[62]

Self-governance

The missionaries trained the native Bhils for self-governance by means of a council and a local committee. All the married men were members of the council. They discussed matters related to their social and cultural life, such as marriage customs and celebration of festivals, and usually reached conclusions by casting vote. Birkett further stresses that "our object is to make all realize that they are really responsible church members, and that the Church is theirs, not ours…and the Council has proved a powerful means of educating the converts both in morals and religion."[63] Regarding worship,

---

[60] Stock, *The History…*, vol.3, 468.

[61] Roland Allen, *Missionary Methods: St. Paul's or Ours* (London: World Dominion Press, 1930). A.I. Birkett, "Missionary Methods. An Answer from Bhil-Land: Letter to the Editor " *The Church Missionary Review* 63 (Sept.1912): 569.

[62] Henry Venn was the honorary secretary from 1841 and became general secretary of the CMS from 1845 to 1872. Eugene Stock, The History vol.1, 370; self-support and self-government were the two main emphases in his memorandum of 1851. The third self was given more explanation in the memorandum of 1861. Max Warren, ed., *To Apply the Gospel: Selections from the writings of Henry Venn* (Grand Rapids: William. B. Eerdmans, 1971), 26; V.S. Azariah, "Self-Support" *The National Christian Council Review* 58/10 (October 1938):536.

[63] See also *Battling and Building among the Bhils*, 74-77. Rogers says in 1911 that in the church of India, native clergy are included in the ruling Church Councils. T. Guy Rogers, "The Church in Non-Christian Lands- Its Problems," *The Church Missionary Review* 62 (1911): 470. But it should be noted that the first Bhil church council was held as early as in May 1907. Birkett wrote: "The Bhils overcame their shyness, and many stood up to speak. We had no Church questions before us, but they discussed the formation of bands of voluntary workers to evangelize the heathen, the simplification of the language of the prayer Book, and Bhil marriage customs… it made them feel that they were united with the whole church." Birkett, Missionary…, 569.

Birkett asserts that in the church all sit on the floor and most of the hymns (*bhajans*) sung are written and tuned by Bhil converts.[64] Thus, it can be argued that the governing system and the worship order of the Bhil church was not very different from their own traditional form of governance and worship. They enjoyed at both places the same democratic nature of governance and indigenous worship.

Self-propagation

Often it was argued that foreign missionaries propagated Christian mission but the Bhil church was self-propagating in nature. Birkett comments, "We hope to train the church to feel that the responsibility for evangelization is theirs, not ours."[65] Bhil Christians were very enthusiastic about evangelisation, as Russell points out, from the day of their baptism their eagerness to carry the message of Christ to the members of their family scattered over the villages.[66] In the Bhil Mission, all Bhil catechists and lay-pastors are under the church council and minister both to Christians and people of other faiths.[67]

Many Bhils, who had the short training of pastoral work, were given a chance to become lay preachers, like Isa Das and Lakhma Jiva.[68] Bhil believers and schoolteachers conducted church services and evangelism by themselves.[69] Hardiman says that by 1958, only one of the parishes, Lusadiya, was under a foreign missionary, Paul Johnson.[70]

---

[64] Birkett Missionary…, 569.

[65] Birkett, Missionary…, 570.

[66] As Bhil married outside their village, so marriage bound village to village thus playing an important role in the spread of the Gospel among the Bhils F.H. Russell, "The Bhils of Central India," *The National Christian Council Review* 56/7 (July, 1936): 354.

[67] Birkett, Missionary…, 570.

[68] The Rev. A. I. Birkett Writes: The Bhil Church, in *The Annual Report of the CMS in Western India*, 1915, 61.

[69] Report for 1929, in *Report of the CMS Western India Mission*, 1929, 16

[70] Hardiman, *Missionaries…*, 187.

The Bhil church was self-propagating in nature and the very reason the Bhils accepted Christianity is because they witnessed a great change in the lives of their relatives.

Self-support

The Bhil mission was initially supported by the missionary grant but soon, when it took the shape of a church by the early twentieth century, they were able to raise its own income. Birkett says that The Bhil Church Council in 1913 received a grant of about 50 pounds a year from CMS (It was largely used in the extension of the Lusadiya Hospital) and local Church contributions were 33 pounds. Moreover, as Vyse reports, the Bhils themselves built all the church buildings with a parsonage like their own houses using mud and bamboo. They also paid the monthly stipend to the lay pastors.[71] This clearly shows the nature of the Bhil mission as a giving not a taking church. Bhils themselves took initiatives to build worship places and supported pastors with their own income.

Educational Work

Missionaries were pioneers in the field of education among the Bhils.[72] Though there were schools in Udaipur, it was meant only for the high caste. Initially, local rulers did not take steps to establish schools in Bhil Land,[73] but soon their

---

[71] "The Mission Field: The United Provinces." In *The Church Missionary Intelligencer and Record*, 28, New Series (London: Church Missionary House, April, 1903): 295; *Battling and Building among the Bhils*, 77; *Letter from the Bishop of Bombay, Bishop Lodge*, Malabar Hill, Bombay to the Wilkson, resident of Mewar, Mewar Residency, 39,1904, P.1 Cited by Jain, "Social Movement…, 131.

[72] Cherian reports that till the 1930s the Christian mission schools were the pioneers in the field of primary education in Udaipur. Cherian, "Contribution of the Churches…, 110.

[73] The main reason was because of the progress and difference of response in the Mission school and that opened by the chiefs of the villages for their own children. Interview with Shakra Bhai Daniel Bhai Hahari. Retired Headmaster, Masaro-ke-Obri, 18 April 2009; "Central Provinces and Rajputana," in *Proceedings of the Church Missionary Society for Africa and the East 1887-88* (London: Church Missionary House, 1888), 110.

concept changed as they became aware that schools would help them too.[74] In 1883, the first school was opened for the Bhils and by 1887, 8 schools were established with the school in Kherwara being looked after by a Bhil Christian named Masih Charan, a catechist.[75] In 1893, after ministering in Kherwara for thirteen years, Thompson expressed his conviction that education had promoted real improvement among the Bhils.[76]

A special one-year training was given to the Bhils in Kherwara for the post of village schoolmasters.[77] Literacy classes were conducted in mission stations for those attending the church. It has been reported that by 1946 all the members at the Kherwara mission were literate.[78] The mission ran one-teacher schools in several parts of Bhil Land and by 1913, there were twelve schools.[79] Sen Gupta comments that parents used to send students to churches to learn manners.[80]

Day Schools

Small Day Schools were opened at six CMS Bhil outstations at Lusadiya (1887), Bilaria (1888), Kotda (1891), Ghoradar (1892), Sarsau (1892) and Baslia (1893) in which about 200 Bhil boys were instructed up to standard six.[81] These schools were constructed with the generous help of the chiefs of

---

[74] A considerable amount of support has been given by the chiefs of the land; some examples are of Kesri Sinhji and the Maharajah of Idar, who contributed a sum of Rs. 1,158 in 1898. "Central Provinces and Rajputana," in *Proceedings of the Church Missionary Society 1898-99* (London: Church Missionary House, 1899), 214.

[75] Kherwara (Bheel Mission) in Proceedings..., 1886-87. 1887, 105.

[76] "Central Provinces and Rajputana," in Proceedings..., 1893-94, 113.

[77] *Handbook for Workers...*, 93.

[78] Cherian, "Contribution of the Churches..., 110.

[79] *Battling and Building among the Bhils*, 51ff.

[80] Sen Gupta, *The Christian Missionaries in Bengal* (Culcuta: Mukhopadhyay, 1971), 80.

[81] "Central Provinces and Rajputana," Proceedings 1893-94,113-114.

these villages, who later also paid for masters and monitors of the schools. Sometimes native rulers also generously contributed towards the maintenance of these schools.[82]

But after 1900, permission was not given to open new schools. Missionaries always tried to restart or build new schools, but were always discouraged by the rulers. Maharaja Dolatsingh, in 1918, argued that the missionaries and teachers "inclined to meddle in State matters and go beyond their province" and created Bhil trouble. To this, the Bishop of Bombay insisted that the CMS missions "have always inculcated obedience to the state." It was an "insinuation, which of course is a hackneyed accusation against mission work by persons, especially in native states, who do not approve of it." Bishop further said, "If anything could be proved to the contrary, the persons responsible would be punished."[83] Eventually, a survey was conducted, which proved that the charges against the missionaries were not true.

Thus, as Niyogi and others argue, education was never used as a means of proselytisation, instead it not only helped many Bhils to take up the profession of school teachers and headmasters,[84] but also enabled them to fight against social evil and exploitation.

---

[82] In Bilaria, the Thakoor of a village subscribed Rs.200 per annum towards the maintenance of the school. A. Clifford, "An Appeal for Lay Evangelists among the Bhils," in *The Church Missionary Intelligencer and Record* (London: Church Missionary House, Aug.1892), 581. Other examples are of the Maharaja of Idar, Sir Kesri Singh was one among them."Central Provinces and Rajputana," in *Proceedings of the Church Missionary Society for Africa and the East 1896-97* (London: Church Missionary House, 1897), 218.

[83] Hardiman, *Missionaries ...*, 99-100.

[84] Sathyanath Bhawa a retired District Educational Officer of Udaipur was a student of Thompson School in Kherwara. He is the present Principal of the School. He says many Bhils were trained as teachers and were the first teachers in all the schools of Bhil land like Jerome Master of Kagadar; Baba Master of Kherwara; Mavji Master of Barna; Mavji Rupji of Godhi, Dheraji of Godhi; Harishchandra Dulgi of Godhi; Sakhra Master , Dhera Master and Daniel Master of Oberi and many other in Lusadiya and Biladiya. Interview with Sathyanath Bhawa, Layman of CNI Kherwara, 19 April 09'.

Medical Work

Missionaries rendered medical services to the Bhils and others from three main medical centres, Kherwara, Lusadiya and Biladiya. But medical work mainly took place in Lusadiya Hospital and the Biladiya dispensary (presently in Gujarat); but as it was the border of Rajasthan and near to Kherwara, the Bhils would make use of their services. Medical services were not limited only to hospitals and dispensaries. Medical missionaries rendered their services also to those who were not able to come to hospital.[85]

Collins reports that even though missionaries were not medically qualified, the Bhils trusted them more than their traditional *Bhopa* or government representative responsible for medical care.[86] Dr. Margaret Johnson states that besides treating the sick, they sought to prevent future sickness through lectures on disease causation, sanitation and hygiene.[87]

Here also it should be noted that the medical mission of CMS in Bhil Land was also not a means for proselytisation, rather it created opportunities for many Bhil youngsters to have their future in medicine. Dr. Daniel Christian of Lusadiya was the first Bhil to qualify as a doctor. Many women were trained as nurses. For instance, Shanti Pandav and others were locally trained as dispensers and dressers at the hospital.[88] So it not only created job opportunities for the Bhils, but also helped them to have scientific treatment.

---

[85] M.Fitz Hugh Johnson, 'Report' Church Missionary Society Report of the Mission to the Bhils, 1946, 7.

[86] The Bhils do not trust anything that is from their rulers. W.B. Collins, in *The Church Missionary Intelligencer and Record* (London: Church Missionary House, March, 1894), 211-212.

[87] Hardiman, *Missionaries…*, 211, 215.

[88] *Ibid.,* 172,196.

Women Empowerment

Missionaries were much concerned about the empowerment of women in India. [89] Many women missionaries came to Bhil Land to help the Bhil women, as they considered "all women in the world were sisters and should support each other."[90] Education played a key role in the empowerment of women in the Bhil country. In 1885, a girl's school was started for the Bhils, which according to Erskine was the first of its kind in Rajasthan.[91] Mrs. Litchfield ran a girls' boarding school in Kherwara from 2nd November 1887. It shattered the stronghold of prejudice in Rajasthan that girls should not be educated and should not be far away from houses, as it was believed that if a girl is educated, she will not be interested in household and field works. But it was later noticed that educated girls were much sought after for marriage.[92] And many Bhil women were appointed as teachers by 1893.[93]

The women missionaries occasionally conducted special programmes for Bhil Christian women, like summer schools, Bible classes and medical awareness programmes, where they were taught the standard of the life and of the World based on biblical doctrines.[94] The Christian missions gave a

---

[89] James Shepherd in Udaipur took great interest in rehabilitating the Bhil women and in his last will, he left 10,000 pounds for women's mission in India. Carstairs, *The Shepherd...*, 250; Jacob, "The Shepherd..., 7.

[90] Robert, *American Women...*, 133.

[91] Erskine, *Rajputhana Gazetteers...*, 83.

[92] Unfortunately, in 1893, the girls' school was closed due to the influence of feelings of castes."Central Provinces and Rajputana," in *Proceedings of the Church Missionary Society for Africa and the East 1903-1904* (London: Church Missionary House, 1904), 226.

[93] "Central Provinces and Rajputana," in *Proceedings of the Church Missionary Society for Africa and the East 1893-94* (London: Church Missionary House, 1894), 113.

[94] "Central Provinces and Rajputana." In *Proceedings of the Church Missionary Society for Africa and the East 1915-16*. London: Church Missionary House, 1916.103.

new outlook for women as equal partners and raised their dignity and standard.

Philanthropic Works

The works of the missionaries have been constantly ignored by historiographers, particularly by those who wrote the famine history of India. Missionaries all over the famine-affected areas were appointed to administer, supply and regulate government relief measures, which resulted greatly in the improvement of its relief administration. All were helped, irrespective of their religion.[95] Though they played a great role in the stabilisation of not only tribes but the people of India in general, in the writings of scholars like Bhatia and Srivastava, the missionaries' hard and self-less work only gets a passing reference and they are condemned for proselytisation.[96]

Famine Relief

In 1899, in Bhil Land, the rains completely failed, causing a famine, which lasted till 1900,[97] causing loss of life from starvation and diseases. P. C. Jain argues that during the great Famine of 1899-1900 the attitude of native rulers of Central India, Bombay Presidency and Rajputana "was highly callous." The tribals of these areas did not receive any help from the British Raj, Hindu organisations or any voluntary agencies.[98] Missionaries did not wait for any help but started

---

[95] N. Benjamin, "Great Famine of 1896-97: The Missionary Factor," *Indian Church History Review* 40/1 (June 2006): 15.

[96] B.M. Bhatia, *Famines in India: A Study in Some Aspects of the Economic History of India (1860-1965)* (Bombay: Asia Publishing House, 1967).54; H.S. Srivastava, *History of Indian Famines 1858-1918* (Agra: Sri Ram Mehra & Co., 1968), 223-24.

[97] *Battling and Building..*, 20.

[98] Prakash Chandra Jain, "Social Movement..., 120. Carstairs also writes that in Mewar State people did not get any help from the rulers, as they regarded it as the responsibility of the local *thakurs* who were the responsible agents of the ruling prince over the subjects of different areas. It has been noted that few officials of the state tried to help but the famine was so great that they felt helpless. Carstairs, *The Shepherd...*, 212-13.

helping the Bhils as best as they could and soon help started coming from friends and other Christians. Mould reports that in October 1899, at the mission compound, Bhils came along with "twenty children who had nothing but skin and bones, to feed."[99]

Missionaries like Thompson, H. Mould, James Shepherd and A. Outram[100] initiated different soup kitchens and relief camps in different places at Kagdar, Umri, Mandwa etc.[101] Help was sought from other mission centres for volunteers, but the mental and physical strain was so great that missionaries after missionaries broke down and had to leave the country, but their place were always taken over by other missionaries.[102]

C. H. Gill reports in 1900 that because of famine the Bhils were completely helpless, as they did not have work to do and had neither food nor water. Many abandoned their villages, wives and children in search of food.[103] Finally,

---

[99] Manohar H. Kala's notes on "History of Rajputana Mission" 6.

[100] Rev. Arthur Outram, the grandson of the famous "Tamer of the Bhils" Mr. General Sir James Outram. He was awarded the silver Kaiser-e-Hind medal for his famine services.

[101] Thompson himself reports that he fed 3,000 people daily on April, 1900. C. Stewart Thompson, "Feeding Three Thousand Daily," *The Church Missionary Gleaner* 27/318 (June1, 1900): 85. "Central Provinces and Rajputana," in *Proceedings of the Church Missionary Society for Africa and the East 1899-1900* (London: Church Missionary House, 1900), 244. See also "Central Provinces and Rajputana," in *Proceedings of the Church Missionary Society for Africa and the East 1902-1903* (London: Church Missionary House, 1903), 227.

[102] Other missionaries who contributed to the mission in Kherwara during famine were Mr. Foss Westcott of the SPG, Dr. Browne, who came from Punjab, Mr. J.C. Harrison who was found by Dr. Browne "in a state of collapse from lack of food" and Browne and his wife both fell ill, as also did F. P. Herbert. Stock, *The History...*, Vol., 4, 221.

[103] C.H. Gill, "The Famine in Rajputana," *The Bombay Church Missionary Gleaner* (June 1900): 1. Described report is also in C.H. Gill, "The Famine in Rajputana," *The Bombay Church Missionary Gleaner* (July,1900): 1. Vaughan Nash, a member of the British Civil Service, who was an eyewitness of the 1899's great famine describes the reasons and effect of famine. Vaughan Nash, *The Great Famine and Its Causes* (New Delhi: Agricole Reprints Corporation, 1986), 79-80.

the rain started when all animals and cattle were mostly dead or unfit for work. So they used their hands to dig up the ground with bamboo sticks. Despite the rains in the year of 1901, the scarcity of food caused much sickness and the people were so excited by the greenery that they did not wait for things to ripen but ate raw berries, fruits and even leaves, which normally the animals ate. This further caused many deaths, since their stomachs were not suitable to digest those things.[104]

During this period of natural turmoil, missionaries all over the famine-affected areas in India took care of the sick and dying, not even caring for themselves. Significantly enough, many missionaries lost lives serving the needy.[105]

During the famine period and in relief camps, where many Bhils were dependent on Christian charity, missionaries, as a general rule, discouraged conversions. G. C. Vyse reports that in 1902, many came for baptism but were told to wait until the crisis had passed. He hoped thereby to discourage those 'with some unworthy motive' and to sift 'the true and loyal from the rest.'[106] But Srivastava argues that during the famine years "a large number of orphans were eventually converted to Christianity."[107] But

---

[104] "Central Provinces and Rajputana," in *Proceedings of the Church Missionary Society for Africa and the East 1900-1901* (London: Church Missionary House, 1901), 267. They ate wild grass called *hama* and their regular crops like maize and *Kuri*, which did not even ripen. The Mission Field, "North-West Provinces," *The Church Missionary Intelligencer* 25, New Series (Dec. 1900): 922. People suffered from Cholera, dysentery, ophthalmia and bad eye. "The Famine Amongst the Bhils of Western India," *The Church Missionary Gleaner* 37/323 (Nov.1, 1900): 163.

[105] C.S. Thompson in Kherwara and in Narsinghpur,(MP) five relief workers died of cholera and other epidemics diseases. Appendix to the *Report on the Famine in the Central Provinces in 1896 and 1897 by R.H. Craddock*. Vol. IV, p.198. cited by   Benjamin, "Great Famine…, 29.

[106] G.C. Vyse, "The Mission Field: The United Provinces," *The Church Missionary Intelligencer* (April, 1903): 295.

[107] Srivastava, "Dimensions…, 224.

in Bhil mission, for example in Biladiya, the boys of the mission school were given baptism only when they passed the examination on Christian doctrine and gave consistent reasons for why they want to become Christians, because the missionaries did not want them to accept Christianity for employment or money.[108] The CMS missionaries continued their relief kitchens as long as people came and continued the relief work indiscriminately.[109]

Different Projects

Soon after the *Chappania Kaal* (Great Famine of 1900), the whole land began to swarm with rats and soon plague started spreading from Gujarat to nearby villages and towns.[110] In order to face the situation, the missionaries conducted several famine relief activities. Outram reports that the conditions of the Bhils were so pathetic that a large number of poor had to sell "almost every stitch of clothing; to these, in their present weakened state, the rains and consequent damp, cold, and fever would bring certain death."[111] So the missionaries distributed clothes and blankets to the needy and the sick. Benjamin reports that they worked selflessly, expecting neither personal benefit nor laurels.[112]

---

[108] W.H. Hodgkinson, "The Bhil Mission," *The North India Church Missionary Gleaner* (November 1902): 77.

[109] The Mission-Field, "The United Provinces," in *The Church Missionary Intelligencer* vol. 28 (April 1903), 295.

[110] C.H. Gill, "The Mission Field," *The Church Missionary Gleaner* 27/335 (Nov 1, 1901): 170. The rats scratched up and ate the seed corn, invaded storehouses and villages. The problems caused by rats were so severe that missionaries decided that one who brings 10 rats only would receive a pound of grain. The average daily attendance of the hungry at the Lusadiya famine relief centre was 1508. The number of rats killed in villages near the Lusadiya centre in December 1902 and January 1903 was 60,484. "Central Provinces and Rajputana," 1904, 224.

[111] A. Outram, "Feeding the Starving Bhils," *Church Missionary Gleaner* 27/321 (Sept 1, 1900): 140.

[112] Benjamin, "Great Famine...", 29.

Free Grain Distribution

During the famine, seed-grain was distributed freely in Kherwara. The importance of it lies in the fact that if the Bhils do not receive it from the mission, the only alternative is to go to the *bunnias* (retail dealers) or *sahukar* (merchants), who demanded three-quarters of the crop in repayment of the seed supplied.[113] Outram reports on 5th July 1900 that each family received "eight to sixteen pounds of seed grain, according to the size of each field."[114]

The rains had softened the ground sufficiently but the Bhils had to hack the ground with axes as their ploughing bullocks were dead. Cattle were also distributed by the missionaries.[115] The Bhils were greatly impressed by the great act of free distribution of seed and it created a sense of goodwill between them and the missionaries.

Food for Work

In 1900, CMS missions began projects such as construction of roads, buildings and irrigation tanks. The supervisors gave women, children and the weak easy work to do, like putting mud into baskets, or lifting baskets onto men's heads and bringing water. Missionaries brought the grain from Bengal and stored it in two large granaries.[116]

---

[113] The grain distributed was not to be eaten but to be sown for the next season. So the missionaries used to check that they should get enough to eat and that they were educated properly not to use the grain that was for cultivation, because that was meant for future."Work for the Famine-Stricken in India," *The Church Missionary Intelligencer* 25, New Series (Oct.1900): 738. Nash says that the exploitation of *Sahukar* continued with all severity during the famine. Nash, *The Great Famine...*, 78.

[114] Outram, *Feeding the Starving...*, 140.

[115] The Mission Field, "North-West Provinces," in *The Church Missionary Intelligencer* 25, Dec.1900, 923.

[116] Buchanan, *Jungle Tales...*, 74-77. Missionaries had to face great challenges as they themselves had to pay for the grain and each bag of grain had to be escorted all the way by armed men, to prevent it being looted by the many bands of looters."Central Provinces and Rajputana," Proceedings..., 1900-91, 266.

Small Scale Industry

Again, after poor rainfall in 1905, widespread scarcity was rampant so missionaries like G. C. Vyse in Kherwara started training young men with different projects like carpentry so that they could lend a helping hand for the mission, while W. Hodgkinson in Biladiya established industrial work in the form of farming for the boys of the orphanage.[117]

Co-operative Society

Missionaries found out that a number of Bhils were still not able to come up in their social status and many were under heavy debt.[118] So in order to free the Bhils from the hands of the moneylenders and to elevate them to a measure of independence, a Co-operative Society was started in April 1906. R. S. Mann argues that "the approach of Christian missionaries involved material benefits which the convert Bhils could get. This encouraged and gave way to the process of proselytization."[119] But it is evident that missionaries followed a general rule of the society that "Non-Christians and Christians alike may benefit by this institution, lest the hope of membership should bribe men to become Christians."[120]

A lot of criticism is made against the working of the Christian missionaries among the tribals. It is established

---

[117] "Central Provinces and Rajputana," in *Proceedings of the Church Missionary Society for Africa and the East 1905-1906* (London: Church Missionary House, 1906), 181.

[118] Richter argues that good rain of 1902 had brought good harvest, but unfortunately the moneylenders carry off the crops from the fields, to cover the interest on their loans so the farmers generally lived in misery. J. Richter, *A History of Mission in India* Trans., by Sydney H. Moore (Edinburgh and London: Oliphant, Anderson and Ferrier, 1908), 238.

[119] Mann, "Bhils and Culture…, 63.

[120] The society borrowed money at 6.25 per cent and lent it to its members at 12.50 per cent. These were very low rates, as Bhils had to pay 75 per cent or more to the local moneylenders. *Battling and Building among the Bhils*, 78.

that even in very hostile conditions in all the interior pockets where the tribals reside, there is always some Christian mission. "One must be charitable to these missions," P. C. Jain points out that "it is only the spirit of commitment which has sustained them to pursue their work."[121] It was reported in 1920s that the Bhils like thousands of others find the old myths and old creeds losing their hold on their minds, and they desire to come into the stream of new enquiry and new thought because of the attraction of a religion which teaches God's care of and providence over men.[122]

Proselytisation or Conversion?

There is a vast difference between the terms proselytisation and conversion. Proselytisation is seen as a 'change of label' from one stage to another, based on inducements and momentary benefits without any necessary change in character and life. Conversion, on the other hand, is the decision of the self without any outer compulsions. It is a change in character and life followed by an outer change of allegiance corresponding to the inner change.[123] Niyogi and other scholars often saw Christianity in India as a result of western proselytisation but evidently in the Bhil Mission of Udaipur, it was the inner convictions of the individuals that made them to accept Christianity. Regarding conversion in Bhil mission, Thompson and other missionaries adopted very tough tests and criteria for the Bhils to accept Christianity. Often the Bhils accepted Christianity risking their own life. When the first convert, Sukha Damor, a Bhagat, had decided to accept Christianity, he was warned by his fellow Bhils: "If you become a Christian your fellow countrymen will

---

[121] P.C. Jain, "Christian Bhils' Ideology and Social Transformation: Search for Relevance," in *Relevance in Sociological Research*, edited by S.L. Doshi (Jaipur: Rawat Publications, 1991), 146.

[122] *The Missionary Herald*, July 1935, vol.131/7, 331.

[123] E. Stanley Jones, *Conversion* (London: Hodder and Stoughton, 1966), 16.

disown you, and the Padre Sahib (Pastor) may leave India." He replied that his "friends could do as they pleased, even kill him" and that "he had his savior over and above the Padre Sahib."[124] This shows the deep conviction the Bhils had about Christianity.

CMS Missionaries in Kherwara always demanded that the convert be self-supporting before he or she accepted Christianity and should not convert to gain access to mission charity. Hardiman argues that care was always taken to see that "those who wanted to embrace Christianity should not do so only for food, handouts or a job in the mission."[125] In 1896, it was reported that one of the young converts separated from the mission simply because he was asked to live in his own home rather than in the mission compound and earn his own livelihood.[126] Thomson commended that "we do what is true and is called manly independence, and we must inculcate into the minds of our people that slavish dependence on missionaries is entirely antagonistic to the spirit of Christianity," and it will also ruin "the Christian name."[127]

Later, the same concept was followed by all the missionaries of the Bhil Missions as in the case of Lusadiya. It has been reported that many converts accepted Christianity there because of the similarities they had in Christian teaching and the prophesies made by their late teacher, which came true in Christianity.[128] Many who had direct intervention

---

[124] Thompson, "The Bhil Mission..., 610.

[125] Hardiman, *Missionaries...*, 57.

[126] "Central Provinces and Rajputana," Proceedings..., 1895-96, 208.

[127] C.S. Thompson, "The Bhil Mission: Kherwara," in *The Church Missionary Intelligencer and Record* (London: Church Missionary House, October, 1895), 771.

[128] The story of Surmal Das is the best example. *Battling and Building among the Bhils*, 24-31. Discussed in detail in the fifth chapter under the title, 'Why Bhils accepted Christianity'.

and personal encounter with God thus wanted to embrace Christianity. Shakra Bhai testifies that "we accepted Christianity because Bhagawan (God) told the grandfather of Surji Bhai Thimodi in a vision that one person will come with a book in his hand, you all have to accept his teachings."[129] When the mission authorities came to know that many of the Baghats wanted to take baptism and attend the church, Charles H. Gill advised the missionaries not to be in a hurry in baptising them but to double check to be certain whether they genuinely desired to be Christians.[130] And this is the reason that many of the present Bhil members of the church are self-confident in themselves and strongly hold on to the faith of their fathers.[131] So as argued by Niyogi and other sociological historians, it was not for momentary gain or proselytisation but due to inner conviction that the Bhils accepted Christianity.

Colonial Support

Niyogi and others (such as Srivastava) argue that missionaries worked with the support of or for the British government.[132] After the March 1881 Bhil revolt, which caused a lot of bloodshed among the Bhils, the missionaries generally kept themselves away from all Europeans. Thompson also thought it wise to distance himself from the colonial rule because it would greatly harm his own reputation as a missionary. He further never interfered in medical work run by the MBC in Kherwara town and only served the people from the

---

[129] A more detailed account is given by the converts themselves to Rev. S.R. Morse. S.R. Morse, "A Visit to the Bhils," *The Church Missionary Gleaner* (2 Oct.,1911): 155. Interview with Sakra Bhai...,.

[130] C.H. Gill, "The Mission Field," in *The Church Missionary Gleaner* 28/335, Nov1,1901, 171.

[131] Interview with Sunil Kumar Asari, Layman, Masaro-ki-Obri, 18 April 2009.

[132] *Report of the Christian Missionary Activities...*, 26; Srivastava, "Dimensions..., 224.

villages.[133] On the other hand, the missionaries took the support of the MBC or the political agent for the benefits of the Bhils when they were helpless, i.e., during the famine relief operation and in medical emergencies.[134] Later, when the mission to the Bhils was extending, the missionaries decided to disassociate themselves from the representatives and political agents of the colonial rule. By 1902, to avoid the growing interference of foreign officials in the relief projects, the mission headquarters was shifted from Kherwara to Lusadiya.[135]

So, as argued by Niyogi and Srivastava, the relation between the missionaries and the foreign administrators in Bhil land was only intermittent and limited and that also was to help the Bhil community in their needs.

The ministry among the Bhils had twofold results: firstly, the Bhils started trusting and loving the missionaries for their service; and secondly, a good number of Bhils gave up faith in their own gods, who, they said, were evidently unable to help them.[136] The people came to see who their true friends were and the motive of such self-sacrifice; and in 1902, 87 converts were baptised after long and careful instruction.[137]

---

[133] C.S. Thompson, "Report on Bheel Mission, Kherwara", In *The Church Missionary Intelligencer and Record*, 7 (October 1882), 592.

[134] C.H. Gill reports that many officials like Colonel Bignell and Major Dawson, the commanding officer in the MBC, used to send one or two gallons of milk daily and would also visit the children to see their condition. They also provided transportation for the grain by means of their some 500 camels. The MBC doctors also provided a helping hand by giving their medical advice and attending the needy. The Mission Field, "North-West Provinces," *The Church Missionary Intelligencer and record*, 25 (April, 1900): 294.

[135] The Mission Field, "North-West Provinces," *The Church Missionary Intelligencer and record*, 25 (April, 1900): 236.

[136] *Handbook for Workers...*, 93.

[137] Stock, *The History...*, vol.4, 221.

Summary

Different missionary organisations have worked in Udaipur; however, CMS missionaries had a lasting impression on the Bhils of Udaipur in general. During early periods, when they did not receive any help from their rulers or caste neighbours, the missionaries gave their selfless love and care for the Bhils. As Egbert De Vries points out, "dignity, freedom, and justice" became the root cause of Bhils conversion.[138] The missionaries worked among the Bhils without any distinction; they helped everyone. Also, the growth of the church was not based on any inducement or momentary gain as argued by the Niyogi report and others but was the decision of individuals based on self-conviction.

---

[138] Egbert De Vries, *Man in Rapid Social Change* (London: The World Council of Churches, 1961), 234-239.

Chapter 4

SOCIAL AND CULTURAL IMPACT OF CHRISTIAN MISSION ON THE BHIL TRIBE

The introduction of Christian mission among the Bhil tribe of Udaipur had a great impact on the life of the people. But it cannot be claimed that the changes brought about in Bhil society are the result of one single agency.[1] In the late 19th century, Bhagat movements and Christian missions assumed historical importance and were able to impact and bring reforms among the Bhils. These movements gained momentum because of the deteriorating political, social and cultural situation of Rajasthan. Both the movements considered Bhils as highly backward people living as sub-human, buried in poverty and ignorance. But they differed in their approaches and strategy. Bhagatism assured to put the tribals within the fold of Hindu caste hierarchy while Christian mission provided incentives of welfare measures and other personal and community benefits.[2]

This chapter looks at the socio-cultural impact of the Christian mission on the Bhils of Udaipur. Downs, however, points out that it is not possible to identify the impact of Christianity on the social, religious, cultural and political

---

[1] Bhil's socio-cultural organisation depends on its contact with several non-tribal communities in different contexts and situations. The media as well as the motive of contact have also been different. The rulers, administrators, officials, traders, contractors, moneylenders, landlords and Christian missionaries, have mainly been the media and sources of cultural contact. Kuppuswamy gives the explicit factor of social change in India. B. Kuppuswamy, *Social Change in India* (New Delhi: Vikas Publishing House, 1975), 93-96.

[2] Prakash Chandra Jain, "Social Movement..., 117.

elements of the tribal society as in a tribal society these elements are closely related to one another. So the main approach of the writer will be to see how and to what extent Christianity affected the socio-cultural life of the Bhils. The writer will also discuss whether Bhil Christians incorporated the old traditional values and customs or whether they underwent a radical change.

IMPACT ON SOCIO-CULTURAL LIFE

Christian mission became an agent of social change among the Bhils through community development programmes like public education, health awareness and welfare societies. Initially, the prominent view among the missionaries was that Christianity through its power to regenerate the individual would surely regenerate society. So saving the soul was given a lot of importance. But later from their ministry experience in India, it became evident that attempts to change and improve external conditions of the individual as well as society are equally important for holistic development. So the social aspect of Christianity was given more emphasis in the last quarter of the nineteenth century. G. A. Oddie comments that the missionaries were increasingly influenced by the more world-affirming, socially-oriented interpretation of Christianity and began to consider more carefully the part missions could play in society and in the temporal affairs of men.[3] Abrecht opines that this change in the prospect of missionary thinking resulted even in identifying Christianity with social change.[4]

The CMS Bhil mission was also started in the last quarter of the nineteenth century (1880) and the social consciousness

---

[3] G.A. Oddie, *Social Protest in India: British Protestant Missionaries and Social Reforms, 1850-1900* (New Delhi: Manohar, 1979), 28 and 31.

[4] Paul Abrecht, *The Churches and Rapid Social Change* (London: SCM Press, 1961), 43.

of the missionaries was reflected in their mission in Kherwara. School and dispensaries were opened as early as 1882. Necessary steps were taken to improve the standard of Bhils through primary and secondary education and through medical services. The Christian contact with the Bhils resulted in a number of changes in their behavioural pattern. It had a great impact on each segment of their life, but the Bhils have maintained the continuity of their ethnicity. In religious and economic aspects, Christian Bhils may differ from other tribal groups, but both the segments, in all probability, share the same ethnicity.[5]

By changing their religion, the Christians did not change their culture;[6] however, it led them to re-evaluate the traditional cultural life and question some of the old customs and attitudes towards people and the world.[7] Often it has been argued that the tribals who swim against the cultural mainstream are Christians.[8] After accepting Christianity, the vitality of the Bhils remained static to a great extent, as the converts were allowed to retain the indigenous elements, beliefs, and practices that did not conflict with Christianity. These elements, beliefs and practices became socially approved, or their underlying meaning was rationalised.[9] S. C. Roy explicitly praises the missionaries for not uprooting the ancient traditions of the tribals:

---

[5] S. L. Doshi, "Ethnicity and Class among the Bhils of Rajasthan," in *Social Stratification in India*, edited by K.L. Sharma (New Delhi: Manohar Publications, 1986), 320.

[6] John Lakra, "Tribal Culture and Tribal Christians," *Sevartham* 25 (2000): 17-30.

[7] Paul Abrecht, *The Churches...*, 13.

[8] Ram Krishan Gupta, "The Tribals in India," *The Eastern Anthropologist* 35/4 (Oct-Dec., 1982): 317.

[9] Keshari N. Sahay, "Impact of Christianity on the Uraon of the Chainpur Belt in Chotanagpur: An Analysis of Its Cultural Processes," *American Anthropologist* 70/5 (October 1968). 923-942 http://www.jstor.org/stable/669757 [17 March 2009], 939.

> The Christian missionaries wisely permitted their converts to retain some of their tribal customs such as exogamy based on totemistic lineage and certain other cherished folk customs and observances, such as the ceremonial eating of the first fruits at harvest and sowing of paddy, and certain observances at birth and marriage which did not conflict with the cardinal tenets of the Christian faith. For their old tribal dances, substitutes were found religious processions, feasts and festivals and congregational hymn-singing… No restriction on food were imposed, nor was the use of liquor tabooed[10]…The educational and other philanthropic activities of the Christian missionaries for the moral, intellectual and social uplift of their converts has undoubtedly been of immense benefit to their converts and have indirectly benefitted the unconverted as well.[11]

Lifestyle

The missionaries were also able to make a deep impression on the Bhils in every aspect of their life. Shakra Bhai says that the Bhils never gave importance to cleanliness and that they rarely ever took bath. A proverb was prevalent in Kherwara that the "clothes worn by the Bhil will see only the rain water."[12] He further says that Christianity helped the Bhils to live as human beings with dignity and taught them to maintain daily cleanliness. He adds that their food habits changed; before Christianity came, the Bhils even ate dead animals and human flesh.

Writing on the impact of Christian missionaries working among the Bhils of Rajasthan, S. L. Doshi comments, "We were stuck (struck) to hear the life story of Jesus and his followers from the cow boys of tender ages in the forest of Kalinjara and Talwara (Banswara District of Rajasthan) villages. The Christian Bhils express their faith in Jesus and

---

[10] Among Christian Bhils, liquor is consumed in a limited way. Jain, *Christianity, Ideology…*, 227.

[11] S. C. Roy, *Oraon Religion and Customs* (Ranchi: Man in India Office, 1928), 338-339.

[12] Interview with Sakra Bhai…,.

behave moderately."[13] Egbert De Vries rightly emphasised that "social change affects human personality."[14] In 1907, Birkett reported that in the first Church council, many Bhils stood up to speak overcoming their shyness.[15] The Bhils were able to evaluate their daily routine, and their personality too started changing as they started speaking out for themselves. They became more community-oriented, and as Manohar Lal says, Christianity brought unity and fellowship in the lives of the Bhils to an extent that they ate from the same plate and drank from the same cup in Holy Eucharist.[16]

Education

Missionaries believed that one of the reasons for the Bhils' backwardness was illiteracy. So, in social and cultural programmes, education assumed an important place. N. K. Singhi says that education of tribals in Rajasthan played an important role as it became "one determinate factor in the processual dimension of social change."[17] Describing why people change, A. P. Barnabas says that "education gives an individual the opportunity, ability, confidence and support to change."[18] This became evident in the life of the Bhils. A political agent who visited the Bhils mission school in

---

[13] Doshi, *The Changing Bhils in Banswara: A Study in Bhil Acculturation*, 144.Cited by Mohanlal Dashora, "The Bhil Economy" (Ph. D. dissertation, University of Udaipur, 1971), 43.

[14] Egbert De Vries, *Man in Rapid...*, 234-239.

[15] A.I. Birkett, "Missionary Methods. An Answer from Bhil-Land: Letter to the Editor" in *The Church Missionary Review* 63, (Sept.1912), 569-570.

[16] Manohar Lal, "A Survey of the Evangelistic...*, 14.

[17] Narendra K. Singhi, *Education and Social Change* (Jaipur: Rawat Publications, 1979), 202. D. Sharma's analysis of Gujjars of Kashmir also states that education of the children plays a significant role in the social and cultural change in society. Dinesh Sharma, *Education and Socialization among the Tribes: With Special Reference to Gujjars of Kashmir* (New Delhi: Commonwealth Publishers, 1988), 99-120.

[18] A.P. Barnabas, *Social Change in a North Indian Village* (New Delhi: The Indian Institute of Public Administration, 1969), 164-169.

Biladiya in 1891-92 commented that "these schools are real centers of civilization among these wild people."[19] The missionaries brought the opportunity to the Bhils to be educated in their native language (*desi bhasha*)[20] and in English. Many of the tribals who studied in mission schools later held prominent positions in the civil services, the army, the railways and provincial democratic institutions.[21]

Medicine

The Bhils began to trust certified medical representatives more than village doctors (*bhopa*). Generally, their belief in magic declined and they started using allopathic medicine; some of them even adopted ayurvedic treatment.[22] Women were taught how to maintain health and hygiene at home and in their neighborhood.

Status of Women

The dignity of women in society rose because of education and jobs opportunities.[23] Education changed the outlook of

---

[19] Lieutenant Colonel J.M. Hunter, Acting Political Agent, Mahi Kanta, to Govt. of Bombay, Sadra, 21 May 1892, Mahi Kantha Annual Administration Report, Oriental and India Office Collection, British Library, London, V/10/ 1543 (1890-91 to 1908-09), 1891-92, pp.35-36 Cited by Hardiman, *Missionaries...*, 106.

[20] Neerja Bhutt, *18ve Va 19ve Shatabdi Me Rajasthan Ka Bheel Samaj* (Hindi) [Bhil Tribe of Rajasthan in 18th and 19th Century] (Udaipur: Himanshu Publishers, 2007), 101.

[21] Jain, *Christianity, Ideology...*, 142. In a village of Kherwara, Masaro-ki-Obri, the top personalities are Christians. The first trained teacher is Robert Kalasua, the first trained nurse Nirmala and the first compounder is Narendraji. There have been a pradhan, seven serpanchs, sixteen gazette officers, two panchayat Sachivs and other government officials, all of whom were Christians. Kamelesh and Latta, who studied in the Kherwara Mission School and Satyanandji Ahari of Kherwara, have been DEOs in Udaipur. The first Bhil headmaster in 1920 of Kherwara was a Christian by the name Singra, s/o Dula Panda. Cherian, "Contribution of the Churches..., 183-184.

[22] Jain, *Christianity, Ideology...*, 142.

[23] Interview with Mani Bahan Bagora, Laywoman of CNI, Godi village, 19 April 2009.

girls and gave them new ideas and aspirations.[24] Girls were sent to school without any hesitation.[25] They became more active in and aware of social activities. Most of the Bhil girls are working as schoolteachers.[26] In 1981-82, Adivasi Mahila Gruh Udyog Samiti was formed with Christian Bhil women as its early leaders. In 1995, the Christian Bhils of Pai, Udaipur, started "Adivasi Mahila Jagriti Samiti," a secular organisation where women are trained in tailoring, sericulture and mushroom production. The Samiti sends the finished products to various cities in India.[27]

IMPACT ON THE BHILS' WORLDVIEW

According to Paul G. Hiebert, "Worldviews are the most fundamental and encompassing views of reality shared by a people in a culture"[28] and it plays a key role in their conversion to Christianity. According to Kraft, in worldview change or transformation in every tribe or society, some of the old elements are retained and some are modified and given new meaning and new places within the total system.[29] Bhil Christians also had accepted a majority of their traditional practices, some were modified and some rejected.

The Christian missionaries enabled them to evaluate their dominant worldviews. As George Oommen comments, they felt that "their worldview was no longer adequate as a

---

[24] M.N. Srinivas, *Social Change in Modern India* (New Delhi: Orient Longman, 1966), 134.

[25] L.P. Mathur, *Interaction of the Bhils with Other Communities: A Historical Perspective* (Jaipur: Publication Scheme, 2001), 72.

[26] Anita Srivastava, "Dimensions of Social Change among the Bhils of Rajasthan," in *Tribal Development in India,* edited by Awadhesh Kumar Singh (New Delhi: Serials Publications, 2008), 292.

[27] Cherian, "Contribution of the Churches..., 184.

[28] Paul S. Hiebert, *Anthropological Reflections on Missiological Issues* (Grand Rapids: Baker Book House, 1994), 38.

[29] Charles H. Kraft, *Christianity in Culture: A Study in Dynamic Biblical Theologizing in Cross-Cultural Prespective* (Maryknoll: Orbis Books, 1984), 355-359.

method of explanation, prediction and control."[30] So they sought an alternative in Christianity. F. S. Downs opines, "At its best Christianity liberated the people from a worldview in which they were socially and psychologically enslaved by the fear of the spirits."[31] Further, while speaking of Mizo traditional worldview, Hrangkhuma says that their communication with Christian missionaries and British administration seriously challenged their assumptions about causality, values, classifications, relationships, human beings, time and space.[32] The same can be said about the Bhils of Rajasthan, who from time immemorial were known for living by killing and plundering others. The Bhils felt reputed and proud to be known as thieves. John Malcolm says that "the common answer of a Bheel, when charged with theft or robbery, is 'I am not to blame; I am Mahadeo's (God's) thief.'"[33] Under the British rule, many practices and customs of the Bhils were criminalised, but they never obeyed the law and often ended up in criminal cases.[34] The missionaries

----

[30] George Oommen, "Re-Reading Tribal Conversion Movements: The Case of the Malayarayans of Kerala 1848-1900," *Religion and Society* 44/2 (June 1997): 67.

[31] F.S. Downs, *Christianity in North East India: Historical Perspective* (Delhi: ISPCK, 1983), 217. Bhils saw Christ's power as higher than evil spirits because Christians do not worship evil spirits and are still unharmed. More-over, missionaries' prayers are enough to get healing whereas the village doctor (*Bhopa*) will not even see them without receiving a payment. Hardiman, *Missionaries...*, 123-137.

[32] Fanai Hrangkhuma, "Mizoram Transformational Change: A Study of the Processes and Nature of Mizo Cultural Change and Factors that Contributed to the Change," (Ph.D. dissertation, Fuller Theological Seminary, 1989), 195.

[33] John Malcolm, *A Memoir of Central India* vol.1 (New Delhi: Aryan Books International, 2001), 526. In 1882, Thompson reports that "about sixty years ago the Bheels had the worst possible name for cruelty. They were then a wild and daring race...considered merely as a race of outcast robbers..." "Some account of the Bheels" in *The Church Missionary Intelligencer and Record* vol.7 (London: Church Missionary House, Oct.1882), 589.

[34] Criminal cases such as their violent and often murderous blood feuds, their habit of rustling livestock from rival Bhil clans, or their collection of levies from travelers who passed through their territories, and mercilessly killing those possessed by witches by drowning or hook swinging. But these laws did not help the Bhils.

taught them that the time had changed and the acts that were considered as holy and just were no more accepted in society. They also advised the Bhils to live by their hard work and earn dignity.[35]

Don Richardson's comment is very much relevant here. He is answering the question, Do missionaries destroy cultures? He says that "we must not and will not destroy cultures... but certain evil in it and...Our task is to give the tribals a rational basis for giving it (evil) up voluntarily before the guns of the police decide the issue with traumatic effect."[36] Later, by the efforts of the missionaries, the Bhils, as Zathangsing Zate points out about the Hmars tribe, understood the sacredness of human life.[37] They also realised that living peacefully is important and that differences between the tribes and villages can be settled peacefully without arms and killing. In 1904, the revenue collector in the State of Idar said, "I marvel at the change wrought in this people. I knew these jungles as good hiding-places, whence the Bhils came out to slay and loot. Now there is peace and quietness." "Nothing," he added, "but Christianity could bring about such a transformation."[38] Doshi rightly points out that the Christian Bhils' worldview has considerably broadened due to their contact with missionary societies.[39]

IMPACT ON RELIGIOUS LIFE

Doshi says that the spread of Christianity has given a new religious outlook to the Bhil tribe.[40] As mentioned earlier,

---

[35] Interview with Daniel Kala Sua...

[36] Don Richardson, *Eternity in Their Hearts* (Ventura: Regal Books, 1981), 492-493.

[37] Zathangsing Zate, "The Impact of Christianity on the Hmar Tribes of Assam Hills" (M.Th. Thesis, Senate of Serampore, 2001), 81.

[38] Stock, *The History of the Church Missionary Society: Its Environment, Its Men and Its Work*, 221-22.

[39] Doshi, *Bhils: Between Societal...*, 22.

[40] *Ibid.*

the Bhils saw many similarities between their concept of God and that of the Christians.

Doctrine of God

The Bhils believe in the Supreme Being who is the creator and blesses them with the fruits of the earth but stays far away from them. Nevertheless, they worshiped evil spirits as they were much closer to them and had the power to cause sickness and misfortunes.[41] They also attributed god with poverty and lived in impoverishment.[42] But Christianity portrayed a personal God who is near and hears the cry of his people, and Jesus Christ as the son of God has destroyed the power of all evil to save humankind. This enabled them to have a strong faith in God and to abandon the belief in evil spirits.

Life and Life after Death

Jain comments that the Bhils got definite answers about life after death. They believed in the immortality of soul so they found Christianity having the same concepts with definite picture of life and life after death.[43] They believed that life is temporal and vanishes like ash in the air. Thus each day was a celebration and they never saved anything for future. They also considered hunger and misery as an integral part of their life. But Christian missionaries taught them that life is important and should be lived responsibly and that hunger and misery can be overcome.

They had strong faith in life after death but did not have any idea of the world beyond death. For them the soul survives in the form of a spirit and goes to the land of the dead to dwell with its ancestors and according to the deeds

---

[41] The Bhils worship evil spirits like *bhut* and *dakan* not only of fear but also to get rid of disease and calamities.

[42] Cherian, "Contribution of the Churches...", 27.

[43] Jain, *Christianity, Ideology...*, 62.

of their lives, they get an enjoyable life or a miserable life.[44] Christian missionaries gave them definite answers, like soul of a dead person cannot harm anyone living on this earth. So there was no need to fear and worship the souls. The missionaries differentiated between heaven and earth and emphasised the confession and forgiveness of sins. Thus the wrongdoing in this life can be forgiven through confession of it to Jesus Christ. This aspect of Christian doctrine motivated them to live a healthy life, as they never had the concept of forgiveness of sin.[45]

Sacrifices, Charms and Exorcism

The Bhils offered sacrifice out of fear of evil spirits. As mentioned earlier, they also offered sacrifices to satisfy their ancestors.[46] But as Downs says, after accepting Christianity, the tribals clearly rejected "animal sacrifices" and "various rites" that were intended to satisfy and appease the anger of evil spirits,[47] because they came to know and believe that Jesus Christ's sacrifice on the cross is all sufficient for their sins and wrongdoing. This not only saved them from the fear of evil spirits, but also resulted in saving a lot of money otherwise spent on sacrifice. The Bhils also used charms and exorcism to protect themselves against evil spirits and other supernatural forces that caused illness and misfortune, whereas Bhil Christians believed in prayer as a channel for the goodness and mercy of Christ. So a total transformation of understanding of the true nature of supernatural and the divine took place replacing fear with fearlessness. Modern

---

[44] *Ibid.*, 70,94.

[45] Interview with Rev Immanuel Damor...

[46] Jain, *Christianity, Ideology and Social Change among Tribals: A Case Study of Bhils of Rajasthan* 192.

[47] F.S. Downs, "Christianity and Socio-Cultural Change in the Hill areas of North-East India" in *Essays on Christianity in North-East India,* edited by Milton S. Sangma and David R. Syiemlieh (New Delhi: Indus Publishing Company, 1994), 220.

medicine and prayer took the place of their traditional sacrifice.[48]

TRIBAL IDENTITY

The conversion to Christianity also involved changes in the social life of the Bhils. However, scholars like Niyogi and Mann say that the converts are bent upon declaring themselves as an endogamous group and at times deny their tribal identity.[49] But contrary to the above argument, Christian Bhils never denied their tribal identity. They kept themselves socially integrated in their community and took part in its activities. They also saw the need of being united with their fellow tribals, and with their help preserve their tribal distinctiveness. It has been noted that most of the tribal Christians, as Frykenberg says, are proud to be known as forest people; for example, Mizo Christians refer to themselves simply as Mizos or forest people.[50] In the same way, Danil Kala Sua says, "We are proud to be Bhils but the local officials deny our tribal identity as tribal Christians and classify us under Other Backward Class."[51] He further argues that after conversion, some of them changed their first names but retained their surnames, such as Daniel Kala Sua, Peter Kanji and Kaleb Kala Dhardara, to show their love and loyalty to their own tribe.[52]

Guy Rogers in 1911 also comments that "Indian Christians" started working along with their "non-Christian

---

[48] Hardiman *Missionaries...*, 242.

[49] Mann, "Bhils and Culture Contact-Case of Social Grouping," 63.

[50] Robert Eric Frykenberg, *Christianity in India: From Beginnings to the Present* (Oxford: Oxford University Press, 2008), 450.

[51] Daniel Kala Sua and Sunil Kumar Asari say that the village *Patwari* (officials) has removed their Bhil surname from all government documents so that they may not get any privileges available for the tribes. Interview with Sunil Kumar Asari, Layman of CNI, Masaro-ki-Obri, Kherwara, 18 April 2009. Interview with Daniel Kala Sua...

[52] Daniel Kala Sua, History of CMS in Bhil Land (Hindi), unpublished handwritten Manuscript, n.d., 5.

brethren" to have a better social life and to build a strong nation.[53] Sunil Kumar Asari of Masaro-ki-Obri, Kherwara, says that a very definite way of cooperation is found among the Christians and other Bhils. They (people of other faiths) see all adivasis as the same blood. An example is Adivasi Akeka Parishat, where all the members of the Bhil tribe take active participation.[54] Shakra Bhai adds that "we love our nation that's why we take part in elections and Panchayati Sabha and we also pray for the prosperity of our nation, Chief Minister, national leaders and for national security."[55] On the contrary, Niyogi questions the loyalty, and fears that because of tribal Christians the security of the State is at stake.[56]

CUSTOMS AND PRACTICES

McGavran's most well known missiological dictum is his famous saying, "Men like to become Christians without crossing racial, linguistics or class barriers." He continues to say that the fear of many is that becoming a Christian will separate one from one's people resulting in men and women, high and low, advanced and primitive, usually turning to Christian faith only when some way is found for them to become Christian without leaving their kith and kin.[57] McGavran's evaluation of conversion proved true in the Bhil community as they saw a possibility of continuity of their tribal identity and culture in Christianity. As J. W. Picket says, the consequent preservation of the converts' social integration too favoured the growth of Christianity.[58]

---

[53] Rogers, *The Church In Non-Christian Lands- Its Problems...*, 470-475.

[54] Interview with Sunil Kumar Asari....

[55] Interview with Shakra Bhai Daniel Bhai.... ; Syamlal, *Tribals and Christian...*, 147.

[56] *Report of the Christian Missionary...*, 131 and 132.

[57] D. A. McGavran, *Understanding Church Growth* (Grand Rapids: Eerdmans, 1980), 223.

[58] J.W. Pickett, *Christian Mass Movements in India* (New York: Abingdon Press, 1933), 22-23.

The Bhil Christians' retaining of culture is evident from their rites related to birth, marriage, death and similar occasions. Mathur comments that certain old taboos and sanctions had to be conceptually redefined under the influence of Christianity. Christian Bhils have redefined the outlook of tribal life as not only have their social disposition and temperament changed, but they are also now more enterprising, development-oriented, rational and calculating.[59]

Marriage

P. C. Jain argues that Christianity has brought radical change in the converts' marriage customs.[60] They retained certain elements from their tradition and rejected others. The Bhils practice village exogamy, as a tribals' marriage within the same village lets down the status of the person. This norm is religiously followed by Christians Bhils.[61] Tribal Christians do not practice polygamy.[62] Elopement marriage, which was very popular among the Bhils, was replaced by arranged marriages.[63] Among the Bhils, the age of the girl for marriage is decided by her capacity to work in the field and to fetch one pot full of water, but Christians do not practice child marriage. Both men and women of the Bhil tribe had equal right for divorce, but according to Christian law, there is no provision for divorce.

Though they have differences, tribal Christians observe all the rituals of marriage that non-tribal Christians observe. The only difference is that Christian marriages are solemnised in the church. In many marriage ceremonies of the Bhils, women wear a top-knot and some *sindur* in

---

[59] Mathur, *Interaction of the Bhils with Other Communities: A Historical Perspective*, 72.

[60] P.C. Jain *Christianity, Ideology...*, 191

[61] P.C. Jain *Christianity, Ideology...*, 191.

[62] Manohar Lal, "A Survey of the Evangelistic...", 14.

[63] P.C. Jain *Christianity, Ideology...*, 191.

marriage. Christians also follow traditional marriage procession and rites before and after marriage.[64] Christian Bhils also practice bride price.[65] The marriage feast and dance and songs remain the same for both the segments. Non-Christian tribals, who comprise the kin group, are also invited on the occasions of marriage. Christian Bhils also pay the predetermined contribution of marriage to the village headman. The custom of widow remarriage is same as that of other Bhils.[66]

A benevolent change in the Bhils was the sanctity of marriage, the stability of conjugal life and a devoted parenthood. Most of the tribal groups take marriage only as a social contract and in many cases, the couples simply live together as man and wife. Christianity enjoins that marriage should be sanctified in the church and must be legalised under the provisions of the Indian Christian Marriage Act.[67]

Funeral Ceremony

Death ceremonies of Bhil Christians are same as that of the other Bhils, with the only difference that Christians bury rather than cremate. It could be said that on all occasions of festivity and mourning, Christian Bhils have the participation from all other Bhils.

Festivals and Religious Observances

Christian missionaries did not encourage participation in

---

[64] Syam Lal, *Tribals and Christian...*, 149.

[65] In the 1906 Bhil mela, Bhil men decided not to give bride-price. Soon it became a problem in the congregations and finally the missionaries changed their policy by the end of 1912 and decided to give bride-price for those boys who were orphaned during the famine. Robert Hack, Acting Secretary, Jabalpur, to Durrant, 22 March 1912, CMS, G2 I 8/0, 1912, doc.11. Cited by Hardiman, *Missionaries...*, 94.

[66] Syam Lal, *Tribals and Christian...*,149.

[67] E.H. Pakyntein, "Changes in the Life of the Tribal Communities of Assam," *Religion and Society* 9/4 (December, 1962): 22; Syam Lal *Tribals and Christian...*, 144.

festivals such as Holi and those related to ancestral worship.[68] But Christians Bhils generally observe a set of festivals which, though indigenous in origin, have been modified to suit the Christian needs. For example, ploughing the field (*orwani*), harvest festival (*katni* or *vadna*) and cattle festival (*gayon-ka-tiyor*). In the rainy season, before ploughing the field, a special church session is held with the motive that God will help the people in agricultural work and bless them so that they could reap the crop. The religious aspects of these festivals have changed and instead of offering prayer and new crop to the indigenous deity, a special church service is arranged on the day and converts bring harvested grain to the church to offer it first to God. Cattle festivals are celebrated along with Deepawali when chattels are decorated with colours and flowers. The head of the family, the father, prays and blesses the cattle.[69]

WHY THE BHILS ACCEPTED CHRISTIANITY?

In the previous chapter, it was argued that momentary benefits and inducements were not the reasons for Bhil conversion. As F. H. Russell comments after his research on the Bhils in Central India that:

> The sturdy independence of the Bhil (had) accustomed him for ages to look to himself for the supply of all his needs, ...and it does not seem to occur to his untutored mind to expect material benefits from those who bring him the Gospel. ...Among the many hundreds who have become Christians in the areas no one has as yet suggested that he be given any help apart from the teaching which he feels is so essential for his life as a Christian.[70]

---

[68] There were some instances in the Bhil mission when lay members of the church were excommunicated for celebrating *Holi*. "Central Provinces and Rajputana," in *Proceedings...*, 1912-13, 143-44. Those who wished to become Christians must first dig up the stones erected in memory of their deceased ancestors. "Central Provinces and Rajputhana," *Proceedings...*, 1903-04, 219.

[69] Syam Lal, *Tribals and Christian...*, 140-141.

[70] Russell, "The Bhils...", 354.

Similarly, Blair quotes that a Bhil will die but never beg because he is ashamed to do so.[71] But Stephen Fuchs says that there are many other motives for the tribals in different parts of India to accept Christianity, like social, religious or economic, though basically the tribals wanted liberation from exploitation.[72] Let us look into the reasons why the Bhils accepted Christianity.

Religious Reasons

Religious similarities and divine interventions became one of the main reasons for the Bhils to accept Christianity.

Similarities

The early Bhil converts saw many similarities between their traditional religious concepts about God, Satan and life after death with Christian understanding.[73] The Bhils believed that in the beginning was God (*bhagwan*) alone and no other. He cast the evil gods (*Gorakh nath*) down from heaven after their disobedience. God then created humans and whatever he/she asks God, it was given.[74] Nirmal Minz says that not only the laws of tribals in India are in many respects quite similar to the Mosaic laws governing the socio-religious life of the people of Israel, but also the teachings of Jesus and his dealings with life's realities have a close affinity to the understanding and experience of realities in the day-to-day life of the tribal even today.[75] Eaton, while writing about

---

[71]   Blair, *Station and Camp Life* ..., 101-102.

[72] Fuchs comes to the conclusion by analysing five different places of conversion, like Conversion in Chotanagpur, Central India, Konds, South India and Northeast India. Stephen Fuchs, "The Conversion of the Tribals," *Indian Missiological Review* 8/2 (April, 1986): 113-114.

[73] *Battling and Building among the Bhils*, 13; Alex Ekka, "Community Transformation and Biblical Faith in the Context of Tribal Cultural Issues," *Sevartham* 29 (2004). 67-82.

[74]   Hermanns, Hinduism..., 15-16.

[75] Nirmal Minz, *Rise up, My People, and Claim the Promise: The Gospel among the Tribes of India* (Delhi: ISPCK, 1997), 29-30. A. Van Exem shows many similarities between the tribal religion of Chotanagpur and Christian teachings. A.van Exem, "Christian Tribals and Tribal Community," *Indian Missiological Review* 8/2 (April 1986): 91-101.

the religious reasons for conversions in Nagaland, says that the pioneer Baptist missionaries pointed out many features of the Christian doctrine that corresponded to the Ao traditional faith.[76] In the like manner, the Bhils recognised the inner harmony between their monotheistic belief and the Christian faith. As Nirmal Minz says, Christianity could offer a viable alternative to tribal ancestral faith, whereas Hinduism, Buddhism, Islam and other world religions could not attract the tribes of India and other countries of South East Asia.[77]

Liberation

The deliverance from the fear of evil spirits was also an important reason for the Bhils to embrace Christianity. The religious leaders, in order to appease evil spirits, asked the tribals to make expensive offerings.[78] But Christian converts were noticeably relieved when they found out that through prayers to Lord Jesus, they no longer had to fear and propitiate evil spirits and they no longer became the victims of witchcraft too.[79]

Divine Revelation and Intervention

Several ordinary Bhils and Bhagat Bhil leaders got divine revelations and dreams about the new religion that would come to Bhil land. They exhorted the people to accept and this became the motivation for many to accept Christianity.

---

[76] Richard M. Eaton, "Conversion to Christianity among the Nagas, 1876-1971," *The Indian Economic and Social History Review* 21/1 (Jan-Mar, 1984): 25-27.

[77] A minimum of five thousand years of contact with Hinduism and at least seven to eight hundred years of contact with Islam could not wipe out the beliefs of the tribes of India. Minz, *Rise up...*, 31.

[78] A.van Exem, "Early Evangelization in Chotanagpur," *Indian Missiological Review* 1 (1979): 358.

[79] Hermanns, *Hinduism...*, 39.

The prophecies of Shurmal Das, Lalu and Surji Bhai Thimodi are some examples.[80]

The Bhils too had divine intervention so they were convicted of their sins; for example, during Bhil Mela (fair), people started confessing their sins. Birkett says that "the most important feature... was the spiritual perception of the evil of sin, which many received during the Mela."[81] In his report, Birkett concludes that the mela had also created a strong sense of unity and common purpose amongst the new converts.[82]

Social Reasons

It has been noted that the Bhils wanted social upliftment as their children were not allowed to have education as other high-caste children. Moreover, they were bound to live as slaves to their Hindu landlords. The Bhils were not allowed to live in comfort even if they had resources. For example, in the Banjaria village, a solider of MBC wanted to build a house with a stone roof; the thakurs ordered it to be removed. This was because by building a house with a stone roof, the Bhil would be equal in status to the landlord. The Bhils were destined to live in houses made of mud and forest wood.[83] They wanted a change and found Christianity

---

[80] *Battling and Building...*, 27-30. V.S. Azariah too gives an account of the Bhils, where examples are stated of Poona and Manji, who helped the Bhils to see the truth in Christ. V.S. Azariah and Henry Whitehead, *Christ in the Indian Villages* (London: Student Christian Movement Press, 1930), 90-95.

[81] Many examples are their but the most evident ones happened in Bhil fair. A.I. Birkett, *'Report'* Church Missionary Society Report of the Mission to the Bhils 1906, 3; *Battling and Building...*, 43-44; Aslo in *C.M.S. Gazette* (Sept.1, 1908): 272. Birkett further writes that 'Holy Spirit was deeply at work, and that the couple of hours thus spent was having more spiritual effect than years of ordinary work or *panchayat* investigations. Birkett, *'Report'...*, 4-5. Hodgkinson also reports that in Mela his laymen confessed their sins in public W. Hodgkinson, *'Biladia'*, 17 January 1907, Church Missionary Society Report of the Mission to the Bhils, 1906, 20-21.

[82] A.I. Birkett, *'Report'* Church Missionary Society Report of the Mission to the Bhils, 1906, 3.

[83] Interview with Shakra Bhai Daniel Bhai...

as the best alternative for social upliftment, as conversion to Hinduism could only give them the status of fifth Varna, the outcaste.[84]

Christian Compassion

Outram and John Buchanan share the view that the Bhils were moved by the compassion showed by the missionaries. Buchanan shares an experience that while he was travelling, he saw a naked old woman left in the forest to be eaten by wild animals; they brought her to the relief camp. Outram says that the Bhils were overwhelmed by this act of kindness as they could not recall Rajputs, Muslims, merchants or Bhagat leaders ever showing such care and concern for others.[85] This, in turn, resulted in attracting many Bhils to Christianity. Hardiman quotes from Dr. Brown's letter that a Bhil came to him saying "I want to know more about this religion of Christ; for there must be something in it to make the Sahibs come and live amongst us to save our lives."[86] Mission doctor had a reputation for being guided by compassion, commitment and selflessness, rather than the desire to make money from the practice.[87] The Bhils of Kherwara were greatly moved by the life-giving sacrifice of C. S. Thompson, who died of cholera serving the famine victims.

The Bhils knew instinctively that by conversion to Christianity they do not have to renounce what was precious and dear in their own tradition and customs. Nirmal Minz says, "Liberation of body, mind, and soul came to the Adivasis through preaching, teaching, and healing ministry

---

[84] Krickwin C. Marak, "The Brokeness of the Tribals in India and Their Future," in *The Church in India: Its Mission Tomorrow*, ed. F. Hrangkhuma & Sebastian C.H. Kim (Delhi: CMS/ISPCK, 1996), 101.

[85] Cherian, "Contribution of the Churches...", 158-59.

[86] Hardiman, *Missionaries...*, 78.

[87] Hardiman, *Missionaries...*, 240.

of the missionaries,"[88] whic0h became the main reasons for the tribals to accept Christianity, and not, as Niyogi suggests, money or job opportunities.

Summary

Bhil Christians, though they joined the church, retained much of their culture. The Christian missions did not destroy the culture of the Bhils. However, this cultural encounter has led to the modernisation of the Bhil society. After accepting Christianity, they did not separate from their community but lived among their own people. They keep themselves socially integrated in their community and take part in its activities. Christian tribals share many feelings with their non-Christian relatives. They see the need for being united with their fellow tribals, and with their help, to preserve their tribal distinctiveness. Christianity was attractive to the tribals because of religious similarities and the liberative acts of the missionaries, which further led to social change. Christianity did not divide the tribes but preserved them. All the tribal churches today are ruled and governed by the tribals themselves, and tribal Christians have their own identity and personality.

[88] Nirmal Minz, "Christianity among the Mundas, Oraons, and Kharias of Chotanagpur," in *Christianity in India: Search for Liberation and Identity*, ed. F. Hrangkhuma (Delhi: CMS/ISPCK, 1998), 32.

CONCLUSION

The Bhils are one among the original tribes of Rajasthan. The Aryan invasion pushed them into the interiors of forests and hills of Aravali. Later, the Rajputs, Mughals and the Marathas not only subjugated them, but also oppressed them. They were inhumanly treated by the ruling Hindu and Muslim kings and emperors. Under the British rule of India, Rajasthan was governed as one of the princely states. They too saw the Bhils as uncivilised and imposed many restrictions on them. Later, the studies of anthropologists and sociologists classified Bhils as Dravidians, Aryans, or Hindus. But the Bhils are a separate entity having their own identity and social and cultural organisation with a unique governing system.

Though the Bhils do not have written documentation of their religion and social structure, they still maintain their socio-cultural identity as an egalitarian society. During the course of their history, they came in contact with different people groups, but Mewar Bhil Corps officials, Bhagatism and Christian missionaries had a lasting impression on them. The British government through the formation of Mewar Bhil Corps in Kherwara provided employment opportunities as corps for the Bhil youth with education and medical facilities. The Bhagat movement offered them a puritanical life and raised their standard to that of the dominant Hindus. But both the Mewar Bhil Corps and the Bhagat movement had only a little impact on the Bhils, as they were not able to adhere to the strict discipline of the Corps and because of their adoption of Bhagatism they were regarded as originating from the lower caste in the Hindu religion.

The Christian missions that arrived in the late nineteenth century were not able to influence the whole of the Bhil community. But to an extent, it helped the Bhils to have a new outlook on their life. Contrary to the argument of Niyogi and other scholars, the Bhil church is not the result of inducements or some momentary gain. It stemmed from genuine conviction. The similarities between Christianity and the Bhils' religious concept of God, life and life after death facilitated the growth of Christianity in the Bhil society. So, for the Bhils, it was a faith journey with new religious interpretations.

However, the Bhils were influenced by the social aspect of Christianity as well. During the famine years, the missionaries preserved the Bhil tribe by giving them care and protection. The mission fed everyone irrespective of their identity and background. After the famine, the missionaries provided grain and cattle for cultivation and formed cooperative societies to liberate them from the bondages of moneylenders. So, when no one was there to help the Bhils, the missionaries lent a helping hand to them, but they never tried to get mileage out of the help they gave as argued by Niyogi and others. Later, social reorganisations and changes resulted because of modern education and medicine. It widened their worldview, deepened their knowledge and understanding and changed their ideas. Christianity gave a transformed lifestyle, freedom from the fear of evil spirits and witchcraft and dignity to the Bhils.

After accepting Christianity, the vitality of the Bhils remained static to a great extent, as the converts knew that by doing so they would not be completely alienated from the socio-cultural aspects of their life. They were able to retain most of their indigenous traditions, beliefs and practices, such as marriage and death ceremonies, as they did not conflict with Christianity. Many of the traditional festivals were celebrated with Christian interpretations.

The early Bhil Christians maintained their tribal identity. They were proud to be called as Bhils; they had Bhil names and always worked for the betterment of their community. After accepting Christianity, they did not abandon their own homes and villages, but lived and served among them. They incorporated indigenous forms of worship in the church. This attitude continued even after the first generation of converts was replaced by the second generation of educated Bhil Christians, who were qualified enough to take over the running of their church, schools and medical facilities. They too tended to see themselves as working for the good of their community rather than for the church as a whole. The education, medical facilities, cooperative services and philanthropic activities of the Christian missionaries for the moral, intellectual and social upliftment of the Bhil converts has undoubtedly been of immense benefit to them and to the non-converts. Certainly, Niyogi and others' critical attitude towards Christian missions cannot be appreciated in the light of the CMS Bhil mission of Rajasthan.

APPENDIX (MAP 1)

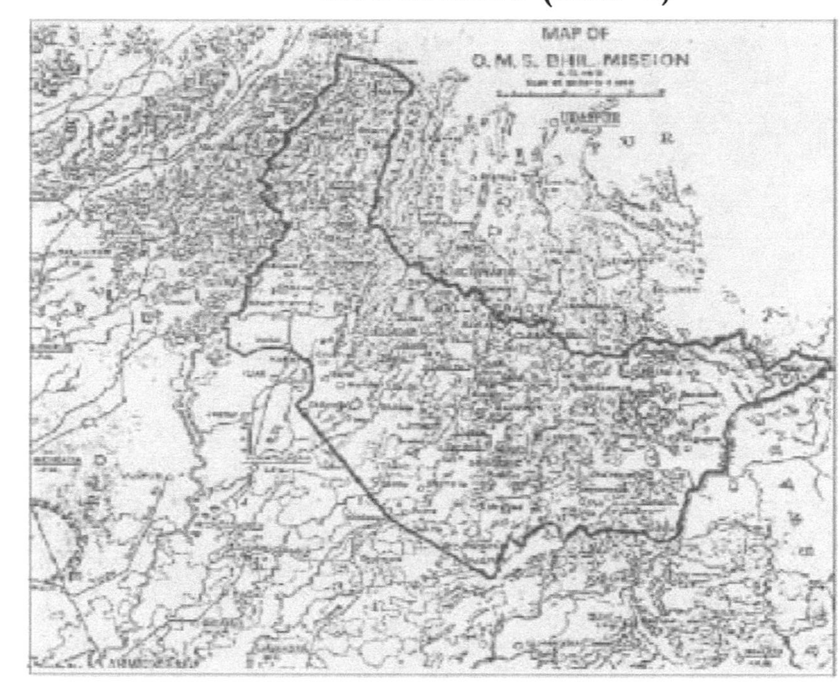

CMS Bhil Mission—An Overview (Source: Daniel Kala Sua, *Personal collections*, Godi village, Kherwara).

MAP 2 (CMS BHIL MISSION AREA)

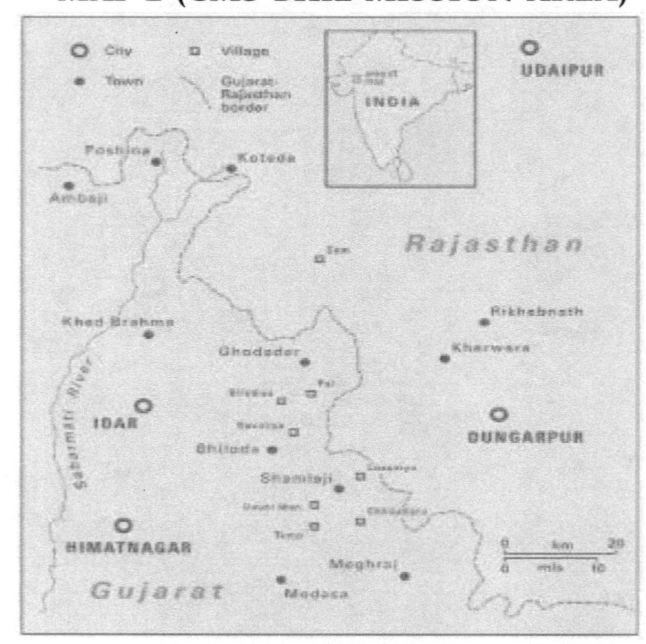

Source: David Hardiman, Missionaries and their Medicine: A Christian Modernity for Tribal India (Manchester: Manchester University Press, 2008), xvii.

BIBLIOGRAPHY

PRIMARY SOURCE

1. Mission Periodicals and Annual Reports

Proceedings of the Church Missionary Society for Africa and the East 1881, 1882, 1885, 1888, 1894, 1896, 1897, 1899, 1900, 1901, 1902, 1903, 1904, 1905, 1906, 1916 and 1919.

Report of the CMS Western India Mission, 1915, 1918 and 1929.

The Bombay Church Missionary Gleaner 1900.

The C.M.S. Gazette 1908, 1913, 1914 and 1916.

The Church Missionary Gleaner 1900, 1901 and 1911.

The Church Missionary Review 1911 and 1912.

The Church Missionary Intelligencer and Record 1882, 1883, 1889, 1890, 1892, 1894, 1895, 1900 and 1903.

The North India Church Missionary Gleaner 1902.

2. Government Reports

Gait, E. A. *Census of India, 1911.* Vol. 1, India: Part 1, Report (Calcutta: Superintendent Government Printing, 1913).

Gazetteer of the Bombay Presidency. Vol.12, Khandesh (Bombay: Government Central Press, 1880).

The Imperial Gazetteer of India, Vol. 25, Karachi to Kotayam. (Oxford: The Clarendon Press, 1908).

The Imperial Gazetteer of India, Vol. 21, Pushkar to Salween. (Oxford: Clarendon Press, 1908).

The Imperial Gazetteer of India, Vol.24, Travancore to Zira. (Oxford: Clarendon Press, 1908).

Rajputhana Gazetteers. Vol. 2A. *The Mewar Residency* (Ajmer: Scottish Mission Industries, 1908).

Report of the Christian Missionary Activities Enquiry Committee Madhya Pradesh, 1956. Vols. 1 and 2. Nagpur: Government Printing, Madhya Pradesh, 1956.

3. Interviews

Asari, Sunil Kumar. Layman of CNI, Masaro-ki-Obri. Interview, 18 April 2009.

Bagora, Mani Bahan. Laywoman of CNI, Godi village. Interview, 19 April 2009.

Bhawa, Sathyanath. Layman of CNI, Kherwara. Interview, 19 April 2009.

Damor, Immanuel. Presbyter in Charge CNI, Udaipur city. Interview, 21 April 2009.

Hahari, Shakra Bhai Daniel Bhai. Retired Headmaster, Masaro-ke-Obri, Interview, 18 April 2009.

Sua, Daniel Kala. Layman of CNI, Godi village. Interview, 19 April 2009.

4. Collected Notes

Kala, Manohar H. notes on "History of Rajputana Mission." Udaipur, Rajasthan.

Kala Sua, Daniel. History of CMS in Bhil Land (Hindi), unpublished handwritten Manuscript.

SECONDARY SOURCES

1. Books and Book Sections

Abrecht, Paul. *The Churches and Rapid Social Change*. London: SCM Press, 1961.

Ahuja, D. R. *Folklore of Rajasthan*. New Delhi: Nation Book Trust, 1950.

Allen, Roland. *Missionary Methods: St. Paul's or Ours*. London: World Dominion Press, 1930.

Ashcroft, Frank. "Story of Our Rajputana Mission." In *United Free Church of Scotland: Mission in India*, Edited by United

Free Church of Scotland. Edinburgh: United Free Church of Scotland, 1909.

Augustine, P. A. *The Bhils of Rajasthan: Burdened by Their Past.* New Delhi: Indian Social Institute, 1986.

Barnabas, A. P. *Social Change in a North Indian Village.* New Delhi: The Indian Institute of Public Administration, 1969.

Battling and Building among the Bhils. London: Church Missionary Society, 1914.

Bedi, Mohinder Singh. *Drinking Behaviour and Development in Tribal Area.* Udaipur: Himanshu Publication, 1988.

Beteille, Andre. *Inequality and Social Change.* Delhi: Oxford University Press, 1972.

Bhatia, B. M. *Famines in India: A Study in Some Aspects of the Economic History of India (1860-1965).* Bombay: Asia Publishing House, 1967.

Bhowmik, K. L. *Tribal India: A Profile in Indian Ethnology.* Calcutta: The World Press, 1971.

Bhuriya, Mahipal. *Folksongs of the Bhils.* Indore: Mahipal Publications, 1979.

Bhutt, Neerja. *18ve Va 19ve Shatabdi Me Rajasthan Ka Bheel Samaj* (Hindi) (Bhil Tribe of Rajasthan in 18th and 19th Century). Udaipur: Himanshu Publishers, 2007.

Blair, G. W. *Station and Camp Life in the Bheel Country.* Belfast: Committee of Jungle Tribes Mission, 1906.

Boyd, R. H. S. *A Church History of Gujarat.* Madras: The Christian Literature Society, 1981.

Buchanan, John. *Jungle Tales.* Toronto: The Thorn Press, 1938.

Burman, B. K. Roy. "Transformation of Tribes and Analogous Social Formations." In *Tribal Transformation in India,* Edited by B. Chaudhuri, vol.3, Ethnopolitics and Identity Crisis. New Delhi: Inter-India Publications, 1992.

________. "Tribal Population: Interface of Historical Ecology and Political Economy." In *Community and Change in Tribal Society*, Edited by Mrinal Miri. Simla: Indian Institute of Advanced Study, 1993.

Carstairs, George. *The Shepherd of Udaipur and the Land He Loved*. London: Hodder & Stoughton, 1926.

Carstairs, Morris. *The Twice-Born: A Study of a Community of High Caste Hindus*. London: Hogart Press, 1957.

Chatterton, Eyre. *A History of the Church of England in India: Since the Early Days of the East India Company*. London: SPCK, 1924.

________. *India through a Bishop's Diary*. London: SPCK, 1935.

Chaudhari, Buddhadeb. "Nehru and Tribal Development in India." In *Tribes and Government Policies*, Edited by J.S. Bandari and Subhadra Mitra Channa. New Delhi: Cosmo Publications, 1977.

________. *Tribal Transformation in India*. Vol. 3. New Delhi: Inter-India Publications, 1992.

Chitinis, Suma. "Definition of the Terms Scheduled Castes and Scheduled Tribes: A Crisis of Ambivalence." In *The Politics of Backwardness: Reservation Policy in India*, Edited by V.A. Pai Panandiker. New Delhi: Konark Publishers, 1997.

Das, S. T. *Life Style of Indian Tribes: Locational Practice*. New Delhi: Gian Publishing House, 1989.

Deliege, Robert. *The Bhils of Western India: Some Empirical and Theoretical Issues in Anthropology in India*. New Delhi: National Publishing House, 1985.

Doshi, J. K. *Social Structure and Cultural Change in a Bhil Village*. Delhi: New Heights, 1969.

Doshi, S. L. *Bhils: Between Societal Self-Awareness and Cultural Synthesis*. New Delhi: Sterling Publishers, 1971.

_________. "Ethnicity and Class among the Bhils of Rajasthan." In *Social Stratification in India*, Edited by K. L. Sharma. New Delhi: Manohar Publications, 1986.

Doshi, S. L. & Narendra Vyas. *Tribal Rajasthan: Sunshine on the Aravali*. Udaipur: Himanshu Publications, 1992.

Downs, F. S. *Christianity in North East India: Historical Prespective*. Delhi: ISPCK, 1983.

Ekka, Alex. "Indigenous People and Development in India." In *Indigenous People of India Problems and Prospects*, Edited by Joseph Marianus Kujur & Sonajharia Minz. New Delhi: Indian Social Institute, 2007.

Enthoven, R. E. *The Tribes and Castes of Bombay*. Vol. I. Delhi: Cosmo Publications, 1975.

Fuchs, Stephen. *Rebellious Prophets: A Study of Messianic Movements in Indian Religions*. Bombay: Asia Publishing House, 1965.

_________. *The Aboriginal Tribes of India*. New Delhi: Macmillan India, 1973.

_________. "Central Indian Tribes." In *Tribe, Caste and Religion in India*, Edited by Romesh Thapar. Delhi: Macmillan India Ltd, 1981.

Furer-Haimendorf, Christoph von. "Traditional Leadership in Indian Tribal Societies." In *Leadership in South Asia*, Edited by B. N. Pandey. Delhi: Vikas Publishing House, 1977.

Frykenberg, Robert Eric. *Christianity in India: From Beginnings to the Present*. Oxford: Oxford University Press, 2008.

Gandhi, M. K. *Christian Missions: Their Place in India*. Ahmedabad: Navajivan Press, 1941.

Ghurye, G. S. *The Scheduled Tribes*. Bombay: Popular Book Depot, 1959.

Gluckman, Max. *Politics, Law and Ritual in Tribal Society*. Oxford: Basil Blackwoods, 1965.

Gulliver, P. H., ed. *Tradition and Transition in East Africa: Studies of the Tribal Element in the Modern Era*. Berkeley: University of California Press, 1969.

Gupta, Sen. *The Christian Missionaries in Bengal*. Culcuta: Mukhopadhyay, 1971.

Haddon, A. C. *The Races of Man & Their Distribution*. London, 1924.

Handbook for Workers: Outline Histories of the C.M.S. Missions. Vol. 2. London: Church Missionary Society, 1906.

Hardiman, David. *The Coming of the Devi: Adivasi Assertion in Western India*. Delhi: Oxford University Press, 1987.

________. "Assertion, Conversion, and Indian Nationalism: Govind's Movement Amongst the Bhils." In *Religious Conversion in India: Modes, Motivations, and Meanings*, Edited by Rowena Robinson & Sathianathan Clarke. New Delhi: Oxford University Press, 2003.

________. *Missionaries and Their Medicine: A Christian Modernity for Tribal India*. Manchester: Manchester University Press, 2008.

Hermanns, M. *Hinduism and Tribal Culture*. Bombay: K. L. Fernandes, 1957.

Hewitt, Gordon. *The Problem of Success: A History of the Church Missionary Society 1910-1942*. Vol. 2, Asia. Great Britain: Overseas Partners, 1977.

Hiebert, Paul S. *Anthropological Reflections on Missiological Issues*. Grand Rapids: Baker Book House, 1994.

Hooper, J. S. M. *Bible Translation in India, Pakisthan and Ceylon*. 2nd ed. Bombay: Oxford University Press, 1963.

Hutton, J. H. *Caste in India*. Bombay: Oxford University Press, 1966.

Jain, P. C. *Christianity, Ideology and Social Change among Tribals: A Case Study of Bhils of Rajasthan*. Jaipur: Rawat Publications, 1995.

__________. *Tribal Agrarian Movement*. Udaipur: Himanshu Publications, 1989.

__________. "'Christian Bhils' Ideology and Social Transformation: Search for Relevance." In *Relevance in Sociological Research*, Edited by S. L. Doshi. Jaipur: Rawat Publications, 1991.

__________. *Planned Development among Tribals*. Jaipur: Rawat Publication, 1999.

Karve, Irawati. *The Bhils of West Khandesh: A Socio-Economic Survey*. Bombay: Anthropological Society, 1961.

Kosambi, D. D. *An Introduction of the Study of Indian History*. Bombay: Popular Press, 1956.

Kraft, Charles H. *Christianity in Culture: A Study in Dynamic Biblical Theologizing in Cross-Cultural Prespective*. Maryknoll: Orbis Books, 1984.

__________. *Anthropology for Christian Witness*. Maryknoll, New York: Orbis Books, 2001.

Kuppuswamy, B. *Social Change in India*. New Delhi: Vikas Publishing House, 1975.

Kuriakose, M. K. *History of Christianity in India: Source Materials*. Madras: The Christian Literature Society, 1982.

Lal, Syam. *Tribals and Christian Missionaries*. Delhi: Manak Publications, 1994.

Lala, S. P. "Impact of Panchayathi Raj on Succession of the Bhils." In *Tribal Ethnography Customary Law and Change*, Edited by K.S. Singh. New Delhi: Concept Publishing Company, 1993.

Mahanti, Neeti. *Tribal Issues: A Non Conventional Approach*. New Delhi: Inter-India Publications, 1994.

Majumdar, D. N. *Races and Culture of India*. Bombay: Asia Publishing House, 1961.

Malcolm, John. *A Memoir of Central India*. Vols. 1-2. New Delhi: Aryan Books International, 2001.

Mann, R. S. "Bhils and Culture Contact-Case of Social Grouping." In *Rajasthan Bhils,* Edited by N. N. Vyas, R. S. Mann & N. D. Choudhary. Udaipur: Manikyalal Verma Tribal Research and Training Institute, 1978.

__________. "Cultural-Ecological Approach to the Study of the Bhil." In *Nature-Man-Spirit Complex in Tribal India,* Edited by R. S. Mann. New Delhi: Concept Publishing Company, 1981.

__________. "Bhil Economy and Its Problems." In *Rajasthan Bhils,* Edited by R. S. Mann & N. D. Choudhary N. N. Vyas. Udaipur: Manikyalal Verma Tribal Research and Training Institute, 1978.

__________. "Structure and Role Dynamics among the Bhils of Rajasthan: A Case of Bhagats." In *Tribal Movements in India,* Edited by K. S. Singh. New Delhi: Manohar Publications, 1982.

Marak, Krickwin C. "The Brokeness of the Tribals in India and Their Future." In *The Church in India: Its Mission Tomorrow,* Edited by F. Hrangkhuma & Sebastian C. H. Kim. Delhi: CMS/ISPCK, 1996.

Martin, William F. *Martin Memorials: Life and Work of William and Gavin Martin.* Edinburgh: Her Majesty's Stationary Office, 1886.

Mathur, L. P. *Resistance Movement of Tribals of India: A Case Study of the Bhils of Rajasthan in the 19th Century.* Udaipur: Himanshu Publication, 1988.

__________. *Movements of Tribals during the Colonial Rule: Role of Ideologies.* New Delhi: Inter-India Publications, 1995.

__________. *Interaction of the Bhils with other Communities: A Historical Perspective.* Jaipur: Publication Scheme, 2001.

Mann, R. S. and Bageshwar Sing. "Tribal Policy in Western India." In *Tribal Development in India: Problems and Prospects,* Edited by Buddhadeb Chaudhri. Delhi: Inter-India Publications, 1982.

McGavran, D. A. *Understanding Church Growth*. Grand Rapids: Eerdmans, 1980.

Meena, Jagadish Chandra. *Bheel Janjathi Ka Sanskritik Eyom Arthik Jhevan (1858-1947)* (Hindi) [Social and Economic Life of Bhil Scheduled Tribe]. Udaipur: Himanshu Publications, 2003.

Metelfe, C. T. "Geography of Rajasthan or Rajpootana." In *Rajasthan through the Ages*, Edited by Suresh K. Sharma & Usha Sharma, Vol.1, History & Geography. (New Delhi: Deep & Deep Publications) 1999.

Minz, Nirmal. "The Study of Tribal Religion in India." In *Re-Visioning India's Religious Traditions: Essays in Honour of Eric Lott*, Edited by David C. Scott & Israel Selvanayagam. Delhi: ISPCK, 1996.

________. "Tribals." In *Doing Christian Ethics*, Edited by Hunter P. Mabry. Bangalore: BTESSC, 1996.

________. *Rise up, My People, and Claim the Promise: The Gospel among the Tribes of India*. Delhi: ISPCK, 1997.

________. "Christianity among the Mundas, Oraons, and Kharias of Chotanagpur." In *Christianity in India: Search for Liberation and Identity*, Edited by F. Hrangkhuma. Delhi: CMS/ISPCK, 1998.

Mishkaben, Marija Sres. *To Survive and to Prevail: Stories of the Tribal Women of Sabarkantha*. New Delhi: Indian Social Institute, 1996.

Mukherji, Mukul Chakraborti & Dipak. *Indian Tribes*. Calcutta: Saraswat Library, 1971.

Naik, T. B. *The Bhils:A Study*. Delhi: Bharayita Adimjati Sevak Sangh, 1956.

Nash, Vaughan. *The Great Famine and Its Causes*. New Delhi: Agricole Reprints Corporation, 1986.

Nath, Y. V. S. *Bhils of Ratanmal: An Analysis of the Social Structure of a Western Indian Community*. Baroda: The Maharaja Sayajirao University of Baroda, 1960.

Oddie, G. A. *Social Protest in India: British Protestant Missionaries and Social Reforms, 1850-1900*. New Delhi: Manohar, 1979.

Ojha, Guri Shankar. *Rajputhana Ka Itihas* (Hindi). Vol. 3. Ajmer: Vedic Yantralaya, 1937.

O'mmelay, L. S. S. *India Heritage*. Culcutta, 1910.

Pathy, Jaganath. "The Idea of Tribe and the Indian Scene." In *Tribal Transformation in India*, Edited by Buddhdeb Chaudhuri, Vol. 3. New Delhi: Inter-India Publications, 1992.

Penzer, M. N., ed. *The Ocean of Story: Somadeva's Katha Sarit Sagara*. Translated by C. H. Tawney. Vols. 1-10. London: C.J. Sawyer, 1924.

Pickett, J. W. *Christian Mass Movements in India*. New York: Abingdon Press, 1933.

Prasad, A. K. *The Bhils of Khandesh*. Delhi: Konak Publishers, 1991.

Rapson, E. J., ed. *The Cambridge History of India*. Vol. 1, Ancient India. Cambridge: Cambridge University Press, 1922.

Richardson, Don. *Eternity in Their Hearts*. Ventura: Regal Books, 1981.

Risley, H. H. *People of India*. Delhi: Oriental Books reprint cooperation, 1969.

Robert, Dana L. *American Women in Mission: A Social History of Their Thought and Practice*. Macon, Georgia: Mercer University Press, 1998.

Roy, S. C. *Oraon Religion and Customs*. Ranchi: Man in India Office, 1928.

Russel, R. S. & Hira Lal. *The Tribes and Castes of the Central Provinces of India*. Vol. 2. London: Macmillan and Co. Limited, 1916.

Sharma, B. K. *Tribal Revolts*. Jaipur: Pointer Publishers, 1996.

Sharma, Dinesh. *Education and Socialization among the Tribes: With Special Reference to Gujjars of Kashmir*. New Delhi: Commonwealth Publishers, 1988.

Sharma, G. N. *Mewar & Mughal Emperors*. Agra: Sivlal Agarwal & Company, 1962.

Sharma, K. L. *Social Stratification and Mobility*. Delhi: Rawat Publications, 2002.

Sharma, S. R. *Process of Social Change among Tribes*. New Delhi: Manak Publications, 2000.

Sharma, Suresh. *Tribal Identity and the Modern World*. New Delhi: Sage Publishers, 1994.

Singh, Hira. *Colonial Hegemony and Popular Resistance: Princes,Peasants, and Paramount Power*. New Delhi: Sage Publications, 1998.

Singh, K. S., ed. *People of India*. Mumbai: Anthropological Survey of India, 1998.

Singh, K. Suresh. *Tribal Society in India*. Delhi: Manohar Publications, 1985.

Singh, K. S. *The Scheduled Tribes*. Vol. 3. Delhi: Oxford University Press, 1994.

Singhi, Narendra K. *Education and Social Change*. Jaipur: Rawat Publications, 1979.

Speyer, J. S. *Studies about the Katha Sarit Sagara*. Amsterdam: Johannes Muller, 1908.

Srinivas, M. N. *Social Change in Modern India*. New Delhi: Orient Longman, 1966.

Srivastava, Anita. "Dimensions of Social Change among the Bhils of Rajasthan." In *Tribal Development in India*, Edited by Awadhesh Kumar Singh. New Delhi: Serials Publications, 2008.

Srivastava, H. S. *History of Indian Famines 1858-1918*. Agra: Sri Ram Mehra & Co., 1968.

Stern, Robert W. *Changing India: Bourgeois Revolution on the Subcontinent*. New Delhi: Cambridge University Press, 1998.

Stock, Eugene. *The History of the Church Missionary Society: Its Environment, Its Men and Its Work*. Vol. 3. London: Church Missionary Society, 1899.

__________. *The History of the Church Missionary Society: Its Environment, Its Men and Its Work*. Vol. 4. London: Church Missionary Society, 1916.

The Church among the Bhils. Lucknow: The National Christian Council and the Bhil Work Council, 1953.

Thompson, C. S. *Rudiments of the Bhili Language*. Ahmedabad: Union Printing Press, 1895.

Todd, James. *Travels in West India*. Translated by Gopalnarayan Bhora, *Paschimi Bharat ke Yathra* (Hindi). Jodphur: Rajasthan Prachya Vidhya Pratisthan, 1965.

__________. *Annals and Antiquities of Rajasthan*. Vols. 1-2. New Delhi: M. N. Publishers, 1983.

Toppo, S. R. *Tribes in India*. Delhi: Indian Publishers Distributors, 2000.

Trivedi, Mridula. *Towards Social Mobility: A Study of the Bhils of South Rajasthan*. Udaipur: Himanshu Publications, 2007.

Varma, Kanhaiya Lal. "Allied Geography of Mewar." In *Rajasthan through the Ages*, Edited by Suresh K. Sharma & Usha Sharma, Vol. 1, History & Geography. New Delhi: Deep & Deep Publications, 1999.

Venkatachar, C. S. "An Ethnographic Account of the Bhil of Central India." In *The Bhil Tribe*, Edited by J. H. Hutton, Census of India1931, Vol. III. Delhi, 1958.

Vidyarthi, L. P. and B. K. Rai. *The Tribal Culture of India*. Delhi: Concept Publishing Company, 1977.

Vries, Egbert De. *Man in Rapid Social Change*. London: The World Council of Churches, 1961.

Vyas, N. N. & O. P. Goyal, *Needs, Facilities and People-Socio-Economic Survey of Simalwara Tribal Development Block2, Dungarpur*. Udaipur: Tribal Research and Training Institute, Rajasthan, 1968.

Vyas, N. N. "Women in Tribal Society." In *Rajasthan Bhils*, Edited by N. N. Vyas, K.S. Mann & N. D. Choudhary. Udaipur: Manikyalal Verma Tribal Research and Training Institute, 1978.

__________. *Bondage and Exploitation in Tribal India*. Jaipur: Rawat Publications, 1980.

Whitehead, V. S. Azariah and Henry. *Christ in the Indian Villages*. London: Student Christian Movement Press, 1930.

2. Articles

Ahuja, Ram. "Religion of the Bhils-a Sociological Analysis." *Sociological Bulletin* 14/1 (1965): 21-33.

Azariah, V. S. "Self-Support." *The National Christian Council Review* 58/10 (October, 1938): 536-543.

Bailey, F. G. ""Tribe" And "Caste" In India." *Contributions to Indian Sociology*, no. 4 (October, 1961): 7-19.

Benjamin, N. "Great Famine of 1896-97: The Missionary Factor." *Indian Church History Review* 40/1 (June 2006): 1-30.

Beteille, Andre. "The Concept of Tribe with Special Reference to India." *Journal of European Sociology* Vol. 27 (1986): 297-318.

Bhuriya, Mahipal. "Tribal Religion in India: A Case Study of the Bhils." *Social Compass* 33/2&3 (1986): 275-283.

Carstairs, G. M. "The Bhils of Kotra Bhomat." *Eastern Anthropologist* 4/3&4 (1954): 169-81.

Eaton, Richard M. "Conversion to Christianity among the Nagas, 1876-1971." *The Indian Economic and Social History Review* 21/1 (Jan-Mar., 1984): 1-44.

Ekka, Alex. "Community Transformation and Biblical Faith in the Context of Tribal Cultural Issues." *Sevartham* Vol. 29 (2004): 67-82.

Exem, A.van. 'Early Evangelization in Chotanagpur." *Indian Missiological Review* Vol.1 (1979): 350-363.

________. "Christian Tribals and Tribal Community." *Indian Missiological Review* 8/2 (April 1986): 91-101.

Fuchs, Stephen. "The Conversion of the Tribals." *Indian Missiological Review* 8/2 (April, 1986): 102-114.

Gupta, Ram Krishan. "The Tribals in India." *The Eastern Anthropologist* 35/4 (Oct-Dec., 1982): 309-318.

Jacob, Jacob K. "The Grain of Wheat in the Bhil Land: Rev. Charles Stewart Thompson." *Cross & Crown* 27/3 (March-April, 1997): 2-4.

________. "The Shepherd of Udaipur." *Cross & Crown* 26/1 (Oct/Nov., 1995): 1-8.

Koppers, W. "Bhagwan: The Supreme Deity of the Bhils." *Anthropos* 35-36 (1940): 265-325.

Kujur, Scholastica. "Are Adivasis Hindus?" *Sevartham* Vol. 29 (2004): 107-123.

Kujur, Sudhir Kumar. "Are Tribals Hindus?" *Sevartham* Vol. 29 (2004): 101-106.

Lakra, John. "Tribal Culture and Tribal Christians." *Sevartham* Vol. 25 (2000): 17-29.

Minz, Nirmal. "Tribal Issues in India Today." *Religion and Society* 50/3 (2005): 3-10.

________. "Cultural Identity of Tribals in India." *Social Action* 43/1 (Jan-Mar., 1993): 32-40.

Oommen, George. "Re-Reading Tribal Conversion Movements: The Case of the Malayarayans of Kerala 1848-1900." *Religion and Society* 44/2 (June, 1997): 66-82.

Pakyntein, E. H. "Changes in the Life of the Tribal Communities of Assam." *Religion and Society* 9/4 (December, 1962): 15-39.

Pathy, Jaganath. "What Is Tribe? What Is Indigenous? Turn the Tables Towards the Metaphor for Social Justice." *Religion and Society* 38/3&4 (Sep-Dec, 1991): 18-26.

Russell, F. H. "The Bhils of Central India." *The National Christian Council Review* 56/7 (July, 1936): 347-355.

Sengupta, Nirmal. "Reappraising Tribal Movements-1: A Myth in the Making." *Economic and Political Weekly* 23/19 (7 May, 1988): 943-945.

Sinha, Surajit. "Tribes and Indian Civilization: Transformation Processes in Morden India." *Man in India* 61/2 (June, 1981): 105-142.

Singh, Roop. "Marriage and Law among the Bhils of Rajasthan." *Eastern Anthropologist* 40/2 (April-June, 1987): 87-99.

__________. "Anatomy of Three Tribal Movements in Rajasthan." *Eastern Anthropologist* 36/2 (April-June, 1983): 117-129.

Singh, Amar Kumar. "Status of the Tribals in India." *Social Change* 23/2&3 (1993).

Singh, Bageshwar. "The Bhil Are Not a Single Tribal Whole." *Man in India* 61/1 (March, 1981): 89-95.

Smith, Ewing. "Mission in Rajasthan." *Pilgrim* no. 35 (August 2009): 19-25.

3. Electronic Journals

Durga, Bhagvat. "Dances and charms of the tribes of central India." *Asian Folklore Studies* 31/1 (1972). *ATLA Religion Database with ATLASerials*, EBSCO*host* (13 Nov 2009).

Durga, Bhagvat. "Folk tales of Central India." *Asian Folklore Studies* 31/2 (1972). *ATLA Religion Database with ATLA Serials*, EBSCO*host* (13 Nov 2009).

Durga, Bhagvat. "The folk songs of central India." *Asian Folklore Studies* 35/2 (1976). *ATLA Religion Database with ATLASerials*, EBSCO*host* (13 Nov 2009).

Sahay, Keshari N. "Impact of Christianity on the Uraon of the Chainpur Belt in Chotanagpur: An Analysis of Its Cultural Processes." *American Anthropologist* 70/5 (Oct., 1968), 923-942. http://www.jstor.org/stable/669757 [accessed 17/03/2009 01:33].

Singh, C. S. K. "Bhils' Participation in Politics in Rajasthan in the 1920's." *Social Scientist* 13/4 (Apr., 1985). http://www.jstor.org/stable/3517516 [accessed 01/02/2010 00:38].

4. Encyclopedia

Crooke, W. "Bhils." *Encyclopedia of Religion and Ethics*. Edited by James Hastings. Vol. 2 (New York: Charles Scribner's Sons. n.d.): 554-556.

Mohanty, P. K. ed. *Encyclopaedia of Scheduled Tribes in India.* Vol. 2, North (Delhi: Isha Books, 2006): ix-xii.

Shashi, S. S. ed. *Encyclopaedia of Indian Tribes.* Vol. 1, The Tribal World in Transition (New Delhi: Anmol Publications, 1994): 41-50.

Vyas, N. N. "Bhil." *Encyclopaedic Profile of Indian Tribes.* Edited by Sachchidananda and R. R. Prasad. Vol.1 (New Delhi: Discovery Publishing House, 1996): 98-101.

5. Unpublished Works

Doshi, S. L. "The Changing Patterns of Bhil Life in Banswara." Ph.D. dissertation, University of Rajasthan, 1963.

Cherian, Abraham T. "Contribution of the Churches and the Mission Agencies to the Bhils of Rajasthan." Ph.D. dissertation, Acts Academy of Higher Education, 2005.

Dashora, Mohanlal. "The Bhil Economy." Ph.D. dissertation, University of Udaipur, 1971.

Goyal, N. K. "Community Development and the Bhil." Ph.D. dissertation: University of Udaipur, 1970.

Hahari, Sakra Bhai Daniel Bhai. "Som Sabhar Khata Christi Adivasivo (Gujarati) [Tribal Christians of Saum Sabhar Kata]." B.A. thesis, Gujarat Vidhya Pheet, 1962.

Hrangkhuma, Fanai. "Mizoram Transformational Change: A Study of the Processes and Nature of Mizo Cultural Change and Factors That Contributed to the Change." Ph.D. dissertation, Fuller Theological Seminary, 1989.

Jain, Prakash Chandra. "Social Movement among the Bhils of Rajasthan: A Sociological Study." Ph.D. dissertation, Mohan Lal Sukhadia University, April 1988.

Lal, Manohar. "A Survey of the Evangelistic Ministry among the Bhil Tribe in Banswara District of Rajasthan." B.D. thesis, Union Biblical Seminary, 1985.

Yadav, Pooran Mal. "Anusuchit Janjatiyon Ke Prati Atyachar: Samajsastriya Adhyayan Banswara Zile Ke Sandarbh Mein (Hindi) [Atrocities Aganist the Scheduled Tribes: A Sociological Study with Special Reference to Banswara District]." Ph.D. dissertation, Mohanlal Sukadia University, 2002.

Zate, Zathangsing. "The Impact of Christianity on the Hmar Tribes of Assam Hills." M.Th. thesis, Senate of Serampore, 2001.